Spirituality and Society

SUNY SERIES IN
CONSTRUCTIVE POSTMODERN THOUGHT
DAVID RAY GRIFFIN, EDITOR

David Ray Griffin, editor, *The Reenchantment of Science:
Postmodern Proposals*

David Ray Griffin, editor, *Spirituality and Society: Postmodern Visions*

SPIRITUALITY
———— AND ————
SOCIETY

Postmodern Visions

DAVID RAY GRIFFIN, *Editor*

STATE UNIVERSITY OF NEW YORK PRESS

Published by
State University of New York Press, Albany
© 1988 State University of New York

Printed in the United States of America

For information, address State University of New York
Press, State University Plaza, Albany, N.Y., 12246

Library of Congress Cataloging-in-Publication Data

Griffin, David Ray, 1939-
Spirituality and society : postmodern visions / David Ray Griffin,
editor.
p.   cm. — (SUNY series in constructive postmodern thought)
Includes index.
ISBN 0-88706-854-5 (pbk)   ISBN 0-88706-853-7
1. Spirituality.   2. Civilization, Modern—1950-
3. Postmodernism.   I. Title.   II. Series.
BL624.G75 1988   88-1152
909.82'8—dc 19   CIP

10 9 8 7 6 5 4 3 2 1

*This volume is dedicated to Harvey and Kathleen Bottelsen,
good friends and the ones who have,
above all others, made the Center for a Postmodern World
possible.*

CONTENTS

INTRODUCTION TO SUNY SERIES IN CONSTRUCTIVE POSTMODERN THOUGHT

The rapid spread of the term *postmodern* in recent years witnesses to a growing dissatisfaction with modernity and to an increasing sense that the modern age not only had a beginning but can have an end as well. Whereas the word *modern* was almost always used until quite recently as a word of praise and as a synonym for *contemporary*, a growing sense is now evidenced that we can and should leave modernity behind—in fact, that we *must* if we are to avoid destroying ourselves and most of the life on our planet.

Modernity, rather than being regarded as the norm for human society toward which all history has been aiming and into which all societies should be ushered—forcibly if necessary—is instead increasingly seen as an aberration. A new respect for the wisdom of traditional societies is growing as we realize that they have endured for thousands of years and that, by contrast, the existence of modern society for even another century seems doubtful. Likewise, *modernism* as a worldview is less and less seen as The Final Truth, in comparison with which all divergent worldviews are automatically regarded as "superstitious." The modern worldview is increasingly relativized to the status of one among many, useful for some purposes, inadequate for others.

Although there have been antimodern movements before, beginning perhaps near the outset of the nineteenth century with the Romanticists and the Luddites, the rapidity with which the term *postmodern* has become widespread in our time suggests that the antimodern sentiment is more extensive and intense than before, and also that it includes the sense that modernity can be successfully overcome only by going beyond it, not by attempting to return to a premodern form of existence. Insofar as a common element is found in the various ways in which the term is used,

ix

postmodernism refers to a diffuse sentiment rather than to any common set of doctrines—the sentiment that humanity can and must go beyond the modern.

Beyond connoting this sentiment, the term *postmodern* is used in a confusing variety of ways, some of them contradictory to others. In artistic and literary circles, for example, postmodernism shares in this general sentiment but also involves a specific reaction against "modernism" in the narrow sense of a movement in artistic-literary circles in the late nineteenth and early twentieth centuries. Postmodern architecture is very different from postmodern literary criticism. In some circles, the term *postmodern* is used in reference to that potpourri of ideas and systems sometimes called *new age metaphysics,* although many of these ideas and systems are more premodern than postmodern. Even in philosophical and theological circles, the term *postmodern* refers to two quite different positions, one of which is reflected in this series. Each position seeks to transcend both *modernism* in the sense of the worldview that has developed out of the seventeenth century Galilean-Cartesian-Baconian-Newtonian science, and *modernity* in the sense of the world order that both conditioned and was conditioned by this worldview. But the two positions seek to transcend the modern in different ways.

Closely related to literary-artistic postmodernism is a philosophical postmodernism inspired variously by pragmatism, physicalism, Ludwig Wittgenstein, Martin Heidegger, and Jacques Derrida and other recent French thinkers. By the use of terms that arise out of particular segments of this movement, it can be called *deconstructive* or *eliminative postmodernism*. It overcomes the modern worldview through an anti-worldview: it deconstructs or eliminates the ingredients necessary for a worldview, such as God, self, purpose, meaning, a real world, and truth as correspondence. While motivated in some cases by the ethical concern to forestall totalitarian systems, this type of postmodern thought issues in relativism, even nihilism. It could also be called *ultramodernism*, in that its eliminations result from carrying modern premises to their logical conclusions.

The postmodernism of this series can, by contrast, be called *constructive* or *revisionary*. It seeks to overcome the modern worldview not by eliminating the possibility of worldviews as such, but by constructing a postmodern worldview through a revision of modern premises and traditional concepts. This constructive or revisionary postmodernism involves a new unity of scientific, ethical, aesthetic, and religious intuitions. It rejects not science as such but only that scientism in which the data of the modern natural sciences are alone allowed to contribute to the construction of our worldview.

The constructive activity of this type of postmodern thought is not limited to a revised worldview; it is equally concerned with a postmodern world that will support and be supported by the new worldview. A postmodern world will involve postmodern persons, with a postmodern spirituality, on the one hand, and a postmodern society, ultimately a postmodern global order, on the other. Going beyond the modern world will involve transcending its individualism, anthropocentrism, patriarchy, mechanization, economism, consumerism, nationalism, and militarism. Constructive postmodern thought provides support for the ecology, peace, feminist, and other emancipatory movements of our time, while stressing that the inclusive emancipation must be from modernity itself. The term *postmodern*, however, by contrast with *premodern*, emphasizes that the modern world has produced unparalleled advances that must not be lost in a general revulsion against its negative features.

From the point of view of deconstructive postmodernists, this constructive postmodernism is still hopelessly wedded to outdated concepts, because it wishes to salvage a positive meaning not only for the notions of the human self, historical meaning, and truth as correspondence, which were central to modernity, but also for premodern notions of a divine reality, cosmic meaning, and an enchanted nature. From the point of view of its advocates, however, this revisionary postmodernism if not only more adequate to our experience but also more genuinely postmodern. It does not simply carry the premises of modernity through to their logical conclusions, but criticizes and revises those premises. Through its return to organicism and its acceptance of nonsensory perception, it opens itself to the recovery of truths and values from various forms of premodern thought and practice that had been dogmatically rejected by modernity. This constructive, revisionary postmodernism involves a creative synthesis of modern and premodern truths and values.

This series does not seek to create a movement so much as to help shape and support an already existing movement convinced that modernity can and must be transcended. But those antimodern movements which arose in the past failed to deflect or even retard the onslaught of modernity. What reasons can we have to expect the current movement to be more successful? First, the previous antimodern movements were primarily calls to return to a premodern form of life and thought rather than calls to advance, and the human spirit does not rally to calls to turn back. Second, the previous antimodern movements either rejected modern science, reduced it to a description of mere appearances, or assumed its adequacy in principle; therefore, they could base their calls only on the negative social and spiritual effects of modernity. The current movement draws on natural science itself as a witness against the adequacy of the modern worldview. In the third place, the present movement has even more evidence than did previous movements of the ways in which modernity and its worldview *are* socially and spiritually destructive. The fourth and probably most decisive difference is that the present movement is based on the awareness that *the continuation of modernity threatens the very survival of life on our planet.* This awareness, combined with the growing knowledge of the interdependence of the modern worldview and the militarism, nuclearism, and ecological devastation of the modern world, is providing an unprecedented impetus for people to see the evidence for a postmodern worldview and to envisage postmodern ways of relating to each other, the rest of nature, and the cosmos as a whole. For these reasons, the failure of the previous antimodern movements says little about the possible success of the current movement.

Advocates of this movement do not hold the naively utopian belief that the success of this movement would bring about a global society of universal and lasting peace, harmony, and happiness, in which all spiritual problems, social conflicts, ecological destruction, and hard choices would vanish. There is, after all, surely a deep truth in the testimony of the world's religions to the presence of a transcultural proclivity to evil deep within the human heart, which no new paradigm, combined with a new economic order, new child-rearing practices, or any other social arrangements, will suddenly eliminate. Furthermore, it has correctly been said that "life is robbery": a strong element of competition is inherent within finite existence, which no social-political-economic-ecological order can overcome. These two truths, especially when contemplated together, should caution us against unrealistic hopes.

However, no such appeal to "universal constants" should reconcile us to the present order, as if this order were thereby uniquely legitimated. The human proclivity to evil in general, and to conflictual competition and ecological destruction in particular, can be greatly exacerbated or greatly mitigated by a world order and its worldview. Modernity exacerbates it about as much as imaginable. We can therefore envision, without being naively utopian, a far better world order, with a far less dangerous trajectory, than the one we now have.

This series, making no pretense of neutrality, is dedicated to the success of this movement toward a postmodern world.

David Ray Griffin
Series Editor

PREFACE

After a long period of relative neglect, the relation between spirituality and social order has again become a burning issue.

In the modern world it has been thought, or at least hoped, both in liberal and Marxist contexts, that social order could and ought to be essentially independent of spiritual issues (an idea impossible for the premodern mind). The bonds of social order were said to be biological or economic, not spiritual. Society was to have a secular foundation. This view was dominant until quite recently. Most of the efforts for social change in Western democracies in the 1960s, for example, were based on secular premises. Sociology and social philosophy, usually in the Marxist tradition, were the relevant university subjects. Social change was to be brought about, if not by physical or verbal violence, at least by essentially external means. Those who held that meaningful social change must be based on inner, spiritual principles were derided or ignored as reactionaries. Even the movement for civil rights for black people, which had been heavily based on spiritual principles and headed by recognizably spiritual leaders, became increasingly dominated by other voices and other principles. The secular view of society won out even there.

But now everything has changed. The viability of a secular state is questioned throughout the world. Secularism is seen as itself a spirituality that is not neutral toward historic religious spiritualities. Islam has become a source of fierce energy against the modern state—a modern capitalist state in Iran, a modern Marxist state in Afghanistan. Christian liberation theology has become a force to be reckoned with in South Africa, South Korea, and especially Latin America, and a Marxist-Christian coalition rules in Nicaragua. Fidel Castro even writes appreciatively of religion from Cuba. Christianity has failed to die in Eastern European countries, and in Poland it has been a central factor in Solidarity's strength. Besides the fact that religion does not die in Marxist nation-states, the conviction is growing that these states cannot be long self-sustaining. In the United States, similar doubts are being raised about capitalist liberalism. Neoconservatives write of the "cultural contradictions of capitalism," and give only "two cheers for capitalism," not three, because of its corrosive effects upon the kind of character needed to sustain a liberal democratic society. They complain of the "naked public square," devoid of religious garments. The religious right has become a powerful political force. At the opposite end of the spectrum, the feminist and Green movements have large constituencies for whom a new spirituality is of the essence. Many of those who looked to sociology and secular social philsophy in the 1960s are talking about the "reenchantment of the world" through new developments in the natural sciences and turning to spiritually-based psychologies. Those in Western nations who ignore or reject these developments are characteristically pessimistic about the possibility of significant social transformation, believing that if the movements of the 1960s could not derail the modern trajectory toward planetary destruction, nothing can. Whereas the archmodernists regarded religion as an "opiate" or an "illusion" with inevitably regressive effects, a postmodern sensibility seems to be emerging for which religious spirituality is the only hope for positive social change as well as for conserving truly important values.

This postmodern sensibility is not a turn to "spiritual" concerns in abstraction from social, political, and economic issues, however. It rejects that abstraction as well as the modern single-minded focus on these external conditions alone. Postmodern writers characteristically address both issues simultaneously, believing that the two are inextricably intertwined. This book contains a selection of such essays.

All the essays are original. Aside from the introduction, all of them except those by Joe Holland and me were written for a conference, "Toward a Postmodern World," which was held in Santa Barbara in January of 1987, having been sponsored by the Center for a Postmodern World and the Center for Process Studies (which are described in the Notes on Contributors and Centers). Holland's paper is a revision of "The Spiritual Crisis of Modern Culture," which had been published in 1984 in manuscript form by the Center of Concern in its series of "Occasional Papers." It is reprinted here with the permission of the Center of Concern, 3700 13th Street, N. E., Washington, D. C. 20017. A greatly abridged version of Richard Falk's paper has been published, under the same title, in *The American Theosophist*, 75/5 (May 1987), 121–32.

For help with the introduction, I wish to thank Ann Jaqua (my wife), contributors John Cobb, Joe Holland, Catherine Keller, and Charlene Spretnak, plus several members of the Center for a Postmodern World, especially Bishop George Barrett, Harvey Bottelsen, James Bower, Gordon Clough, Anne Corner, Olive Franklin, Margaret Getman, Edward Gillis, Mark Hamilton, Anne Sutherland Howard, Frank Kelly, Charles Muses, and librarian and research assistant Erline Goodell, who provided bibliographic help. My other intellectual debts are indicated in the notes to the introduction. I want to call special attention to the great book by Stephen Turner and Regis Factor, *Max Weber and the Dispute over Reason and Value.* This is useful scholarship at its best. On the practical side, I received yeoperson assistance from my secretary in Claremont, Geneva Villegas. I am grateful to President Richard C. Cain and the trustees of the School of Theology at Claremont for providing a leave of absence, and to John Cobb and Nancy Howell of the Center for Process Studies for making it possible for me to be absent for a year. Finally, I continue to be thankful to editor William Eastman of SUNY Press and to his staff, especially production editor Elizabeth Moore.

1

INTRODUCTION: POSTMODERN SPIRITUALITY AND SOCIETY

David Ray Griffin

This book, the second in the series, deals with the nature of a postmodern *world*. It stands in contrast thereby with the first and third volumes, which deal with the nature of a postmodern *worldview*, in terms of science and theology, respectively. This volume is concerned with what it would mean, for persons and societies, to live in terms of some such worldview.

For many people, the term *spirituality* has otherworldly connotations and implies some form of religious discipline. The term is used here in a broad sense, however, to refer to the ultimate values and meanings in terms of which we live, whether they be otherworldly or very worldly ones, and whether or not we consciously try to increase our commitment to those values and meanings. The term does have religious connotations, in that one's ultimate values and meanings reflect some presupposition as to what is *holy*, that is, of ultimate importance. But the presupposed holy can be something very worldly, such as power, sexual energy, or success. Spirituality in this broad sense is not an optional quality which we might elect not to have. Everyone embodies a spirituality, even if it be a nihilistic or materialistic

1

spirituality. It is also, of course, customary to use *spirituality* in a stricter sense for a way of life oriented around an ultimate meaning and around values other than power, pleasure, and possession. When *spirituality* is used in this stricter sense, nihilism and materialism are pseudospiritualities, even antispiritualities, as Joe Holland calls them herein. But *spirituality* as used here refers to a person's ultimate values and commitments, regardless of their content.

The relation between a society and its members' spirituality is reciprocal. A society's customs and laws, on the one hand, reflect the spirituality of its members. The spirituality of the members, on the other hand, is largely shaped by the nature of the society. This "largely" is never, however, "totally." In spite of archmodernist B. F. Skinner's denial of "freedom and dignity," [1] we are not simply the products of our natural and social environments. We are, to be sure, deeply constituted by our relations to these environments. But in each moment, we create ourselves out of these relations in terms of our desires, purposes, meanings, and values—in short, out of our spirituality. Because of this element of autonomy, individuals are not only shaped by their society; they can shape it in return. In stating this twofold position—that individuals are internally constituted by their social relations, and that they are nevertheless not totally determined by them—I have already rejected a modern for a postmodern viewpoint.

This introduction places this volume's essays within some of the larger discussion of the meaning of modernity and of what it would mean to be postmodern persons living in a postmodern world. I hope thereby to enable the distinctive contributions of each essay to stand out more clearly.

The first section explores the nature of modern spirituality; the second, the nature of modern society. The third and fourth sections deal with postmodern spirituality and postmodern society, respectively.

Because the main concern here is with a shift from a modern to a postmodern spirituality and society, the discussion focuses more on points of contrast than on points of continuity, even though the latter are equally important. To summarize some of the main points of contrast in advance: Modern spirituality began as a dualistic, supernaturalistic spirituality, and ended as a pseudo- or antispirituality; postmodernity involves a return to a genuine spirituality that incorporates elements from premodern spiritualities. Because postmodern spirituality is not simply a return to a premodern spirituality, however, the type of society it legitimates must be different from premodern as well as from modern societies. Although this postmodern society will retain and expand many features of the modern world, it will reverse modernity's individualism and nationalism, its subordination of humanity to the machine, its subordination of social, moral, aesthetic, religious, and ecological concerns to economic interests, and it will transcend both of the modern economic systems.

I. MODERN SPIRITUALITY

Virtually all interpreters of modernity emphasize the centrality of individualism.[2] Philosophically, individualism means the denial that the human self is internally related to other things, that is, that the individual person is significantly constituted by his or her relations to other people, to institutions, to nature, to the past, even perhaps to a divine creator. Descartes expressed this individualism most succinctly in his definition of a substance—of which the human soul was a prime example—as that which requires nothing but itself to be itself.

Why this individualistic notion of the self became accepted in early modernity can be explained in various ways. Some interpreters see it as a final outworking of the human tendency to understand ourselves by analogy with the divine reality, combined with the notion of divinity as a completely independent, impassible being.[3] Others attribute growing individualism primarily to centuries of Christian influence (without invoking the classical Christian idea of God as fully independent in particular).[4] Other interpreters focus on the new idea of nature as composed of essentially independent atoms, and see the individualistic psychology and spirituality as developing out of a tendency to understand ourselves by analogy with natural entities. Still others reverse this process, explaining the atomistic understanding of nature in terms of the early modern desire to convince people that they had no essential connections to traditional institutions, such as the guild, the rural community, or the church.[5] In this case, the individualistic spirituality would have to be explained in some other terms, such as the dynamics of the emerging capitalistic order, which required the existence of a large pool of free labor, that is, of people who no longer had their subsistence farms or traditional trades and were hence forced to sell their labor to the owners of land and industries.[6]

Regardless of how it is explained, however, modernity has involved a major shift from a communal to an individualistic self-understanding. Rather than seeing society or the community as having primacy, with the (only partly autonomous) "individual" as its product, modernity regards the society as a mere aggregate of freestanding individuals who have joined together voluntarily to achieve certain purposes. Modernity has to admit, of course, that a few relationships, especially to one's parents, are essential; but these relationships are seen as exceptional. The emphasis, pointing to an ideal, has been on one's essential independence from others.

Whereas *individualism* is generally used to characterize modern spirituality in relation to society and its institutions, the term *dualism* points to modern spirituality's relationship with the natural world, at least in the first phase of modernity. The human soul, mind, or self was felt to be completely different from the rest of the creation. Given the mechanistic view of nature adopted by modernity, this absolute difference was required for an affirmation of human freedom. Insofar as dualism proclaimed the essential independence of the soul from the body, it was simply individualism in relation to nature. In its dimension of regarding nature as devoid of all sentience, it provided the ideological justification for modernity's drive toward unlimited domination and exploitation of nature, including all other living species.[7] This drive to dominate, subdue, master, and control nature is one of the central features of modern spirituality.

Modernity's radical individualism and dualistic domination are unique in the history of human culture; equally unique is modernity's relation to time.[8] The modern "myth of progress" denigrates the past, the traditional, by speaking of modernity as "enlightenment" and the past as "dark ages," and by contrasting "modern science" with primitive and medieval "superstition." The myth of progress is perhaps best expressed by Auguste Comte's periodization of human history into the ages of theology, metaphysics, and science, a periodization that is still widely presupposed in educated circles. Another dimension of the modern orientation is what Peter Berger calls *futurism*, the tendency to find almost all of the present's meaning in its relation to the future rather than to the past, which in practice means an indifferent forgetfulness of the past, a cutting of ties to it, and a fascination with novelty. This radical antitraditionalism of modernity is one more dimension of its individualism, in that the relation to the past is not regarded as constitutive of the present.

Modern spirituality is also distinguished from previous modes of human existence through its relation to divinity or holiness. The divine reality for the Middle Ages was both transcendent and immanent. Protestantism moved away from divine immanence and toward pure transcendence—for example, by reducing the number of sacraments, by moving toward a purely emblematic interpretation of the eucharist, by rejecting icons, saints, and post-Biblical miracles, and by rejecting infused grace in favor of imputed justification. Early modern theological scientists (including Catholics such as Mersenne and Descartes as well as Protestants such as Boyle and Newton) carried this tendency to an extreme, so that God was wholly outside the world. The mechanistic picture of nature, basic to the mind-and-nature dualism mentioned above, was a denial of divine immanence in nature. But any natural immanence of God in the human mind was also denied, mainly through the "sensationist" doctrine of experience, according to which nothing can be present in the mind except what enters through the physical senses. Because these senses cannot perceive God, God cannot be naturally present in the human mind. God could be known through a supernatural revelation, of course, as long as people accepted supernaturalistic theism, according to which God created the world out of absolute nothingness and can interrupt the laws of nature at will.

Once supernaturalism had changed from theism to deism, according to which God does not intervene after the initial creation, God could be known only by inference from the created order or through an innate, implanted idea. A divine reality was a matter of belief, not direct experience: all mysticism or "enthusiasm" was proscribed. Life for the most part was to be lived as if there were no God. Religion, to the degree that it survived at all, was increasingly restricted to a private affair; the public realm was, in effect, virtually godless.

Deism was a halfway house between theism and complete atheism. The move to complete atheism is at the root of the second phase of modern spirituality. This move completes the transition to *secularism*, which is usually lifted up as one of the chief characteristics of modernity. Contrary to widespread belief, however, secularism does not involve any decline in religiosity; it only means a transference of religious devotion from one kind of religious object to another—from one that transcends the world, at least in part, to one that is fully worldly, that is, secular. This religiosity can be expressed in Fascism, Communism, Nationalism, Scientism, Aestheticism, Nuclearism, or in several other secular religions, sometimes called quasi-religions.

One of the main results of this transition from supernaturalism to secularism involved the relation of human beings to moral and aesthetic norms. This transition was the ultimate step in the "disenchantment of the world" of which Max Weber spoke. Although this disenchantment involved several dimensions, beginning with the rejection of myth and magic, for Weber it meant primarily the denial that the world contains objective moral and aesthetic norms, at least any of which we can obtain knowledge.[9] The modern limitation of perception to sensory perception ruled out nonsensory, "intuitive" knowledge of norms. Deism had allowed aesthetic and especially moral norms to be known through innate ideas, thought to have been instilled in us by the deistic author of nature, a position accepted by Thomas Jefferson.[10] But after even this deistic creator was rejected, no basis remained for believing that we could have genuine knowledge of ethical or aesthetic norms.

At least one such norm might seem to be implicit in the doctrine of the human soul. Because we are experiencing, purposive beings, who are ends in ourselves, not mere instruments for the ends of others, it can be argued that we should treat other human beings by analogy as ends in themselves. The ethical stance of humanism, or humanitarianism, would hence be implied by modern dualism.

Closely related to the transition from supernaturalism to atheism, however, was a transition from dualism to materialism, according to which human beings have no soul or mind setting them apart from the rest of nature. The modern interpretation of nature justified its exploitation. Given this modern meaning of *nature* , the materialistic assertion that human beings are fully natural removes the theoretical basis for regarding them with special respect. They are simply one more part of the deterministic, meaningless sequence of events. No reason can be given for treating them as ends in themselves rather than simply as means for the ends of the most powerful.

The result of the transition from supernaturalistic dualism to atheistic materialism is a position that can variously be called nihilism, relativism, determinism, scientism, positivism, instrumental rationality, and decisionism. *Nihilism* is the denial of anything of ultimate value or meaning, hence of all objective norms as to how we ought to live. The term *relativism* indicates that all value-judgments are relative to some limited perspective and purpose, that no standpoint exists from which some normative assertions can be said to be really (objectively) better than others. *Determinism* means that everything occurs as it must; the idea that human choices can change the course of history is therefore an illusion. *Scientism* and *positivism* mean that the method of the modern natural sciences, which limit themselves to ascertaining facts (as opposed to values), is the only method for ascertaining truth. Theology, metaphysics, ethics, and aesthetics, in other words, do not produce *cognitive* assertions, that is, ones that are capable of being true or false. The idea—which to Weber lay at the heart of modernity— that rationality is limited to instrumental rationality (*Zweckrationalität*)[11] says that reason is incapable of dealing with ends or values, that it can answer only the question how best to achieve ends that are arrived at on some nonrational basis. *Decisionism* is the doctrine that ultimate ends or values can be accepted only on the basis of an nonrational decision.[12] One may decide for Nationalism, another for Humanism, another for Art-as-Religion, another for Christianity, another for Communism, and another for Fascism, but one can provide no rational basis for saying that one's own decision is in any sense better than the others.

Modern spirituality can also be discussed in terms of a new attitude toward self-interest in relation to morality. Moral norms have their function in relation to our power to make decisions, through which we shape our own lives and influence the world beyond us. Moral norms generally stand in some tension with self-interest as usually understood, and the most admirable lives have traditionally been ones in which self-interest had either been subordinated to or shaped by such norms (leaving aside those exceptional lives in which self-interest is so radically transformed by other-interest that such norms are superfluous).

One of the unique features of modern spirituality is that it has come to regard self-interest (as usually understood) as an acceptable basis for at least one dimension of life, that is, the economic dimension.[13] This allowance for self-interest to run unbridled by morality in the marketplace was originally justified morally.[14] It was argued that an economic system based upon self-interest would, in general, bring about more benefits to everyone than a system based upon more moral behavior on the part of individuals. This idea was classically stated in Bernard Mandeville's *The Fable of the Bees*, which was subtitled *Private Vices, Public Benefits*. This idea became widely influential through the *Wealth of Nations* by Adam Smith, who, however much he may have detested Mandeville's doctrine in general, did incorporate it for the economic realm of life in his famous doctrine of "the invisible hand."[15]

In more recent modernity, this acceptance of self-interest as the operating principle of life has been extended to many other, if not all, dimensions of human life, so much so that "neoconservative" defenders of capitalistic democracy fear that this late modern spirituality lacks the virtues (such as self-restraint, concern for the general good, and nationalistic patriotism) necessary to sustain this system. [16] Hence, late modern spirituality is seen as not only destructive of individuals, because of its nihilism, but destructive of modern society as well.

In late modern spirituality, self-interest seems to have an altered relation to time. Early modern spirituality's relation to time was characterized above as a "futurism" in which any positive relation to the past was virtually lost. All attention was given to the future—making and saving money for one's later years, one's children and grandchildren, making the world a better place, and—most ambitiously—bringing about "the kingdom of heaven on earth." The past and its ways were rejected out of the conviction that the future would be better. This spirituality often evoked the protest that modern people were so heavily oriented toward the future that they did not live in the present. In late modern spirituality, however, the positive relation to the future seems to be disappearing as well, leaving the "narcissistic personality" wrapped up in concern for immediate gratification.

This development is the ultimate example of individualism, in that self-interest no longer involves an interest in one's posterity. [17] To some extent, this development is surely the product of the environmental and nuclear crises. Having decided that the modern economic-technological-militaristic trajectory cannot possibly be changed, many people have lost confidence that there will be any posterity. [18] When combined with a previous loss of faith in any traditional form of religious immortality, this loss of confidence in the future of humanity leaves little basis for people's interest to be extended beyond the rather immediate present.

Closely related to the question of self-interest is the question of how we shape our ability to exert power on other beings, especially other sentient, self-determining beings. Because such beings are ends in themselves, traditional spiritualities presumed that the use of coercive power, which inflicts pain on them and limits their freedom for self-determination, required justification in terms of overriding considerations. Modernity, however, has undermined this presumption. The "death of God" is taken to mean that no norms exist to restrain our will-to-power. [19] The ideology of Social Darwinism even gave a moral argument for this immorality, saying that the human race can only be improved through a system of competitive individualism in which the "unfit" are allowed to die or become subservient.[20] Late modern spirituality has, in sum, felt that no reason exists, beyond the power of others, to restrain one's own use of power in striving to realize one's interests: "Might makes right."

Modern spirituality is described from yet another angle as a one-sidedly masculine spirituality. The wholly transcendent, omnipotent God of first-stage modernity was, from a history-of-religions viewpoint, a reversion to the masculine sky-god; divine immanence in nature, which has always been identified with the feminine side of divinity, was wholly rejected. The dualism of mind and nature, with the attribution of consciousness, self-movement, and intrinsic value only to the human mind, justified the superiority not only of "man" to nature but also of male to female. The theologian-scientists of the seventeenth century rather clearly said that they were developing a "masculine" science.[21] The preference for contract over custom, of sense-perception over intuition, of objectivity over subjectivity, and of facts over values can all be seen as expressions of an elevation of maleness over femaleness. Those who make these points are not claiming, of course, that modernity invented androcentrism and patriarchy, because these have existed for thousands of years and in most cultures. Nor are they claiming that women have not achieved some significant freedoms in the modern world, in comparison with most traditional societies. The points made (by Catherine Keller and Charlene Spretnak herein) are that early modernity reaffirmed and in some respects intensified an androcentric outlook and masculinist spirituality, that this one-sided outlook with its spirituality has continued to be effective to this day, and that its embodiment in modern technologies of mass destruction makes it more dangerous than ever.

A point of clarification before continuing: to describe the above features as characteristic of modern spirituality is not to say that all or even the majority of the people in modern society are thus describable, or even that the most modern individuals embody these features unambiguously. It is to say, instead, that modern ideology and social policy exert a steady pressure on people to develop these features, and that these features are increasingly embodied—in more people and with more completeness—in each generation. The same is true of the features of modern society described in the following section.

II. Modern Society

The previous section discussed modernity primarily from the point of view of the individual, the psychologist, the philosopher, the theologian, and the historian of ideas; this section discusses it more from the point of view of society, the sociologist, the political philosopher, and the economic and social historian. Just as some sociological comments were included in the previous section, however, further comments about modern spirituality are contained in this section.

Individualism, which was discussed in the previous section in terms of the philosophical question of internal relatedness, involves, from the sociological point of view, primarily the destruction of small, intimate, organic communities and institutions in a process of *centralization*. Economically this centralization is *industrialization* (sometimes capitalist, sometimes socialist); sociologically it is *urbanization*; politically it is reflected in *nationalism*. This movement has been described most influentially by Ferdinand Tönnies as the transition from community (*Gemeinschaft*) to aggregative society (*Gesellschaft*). It has also been called the transition from a customary to a contractual society, or from a society based on tradition to one based on rational calculation.[22] The main point is that most of those structures in which people had intimate, face-to-face relations, and which had answered most of life's questions, were destroyed or weakened, so that the individual's "social relations" became increasingly restricted to large, impersonal groups—the large factory, the national economy, the large city, and the nation-state—in which only a very abstract portion of one's life is involved. For example, in a discussion of patriotism, Peter Berger says: "What is peculiarly modern is that the nation-state (itself a recent apparition on the stage of history) has become the major focus of patriotic sentiment."[23] A better term than either *individualism* or *centralization* might be *dichotomization*. As Berger says: "Modernization brings about a novel dichotomization of social life . . . between megastructures and private life." Modernization destroys those "mediating structures" that "stand between the individual in his private sphere and the large institutions of the public sphere."[24] Berger describes the effect of the transition from community to impersonal society on modern spirituality:

> Community was real and all-embracing, for better or for worse. The individual was thus rarely, if ever, thrown back upon himself. . . . Modernity, by contrast, is marked by homelessness. The forces of modernization have descended like a gigantic steel hammer upon all the old communal institutions—clan, village, tribe, regions. . . . It is hardly surprising that this transformation caused severe discontents.[25]

Emile Durkheim discussed those discontents in terms of anomie and suicide.[26] More recently, Christopher Lasch has described them in terms of the "narcissistic" personality, mentioned earlier.[27]

Another inclusive term used to describe modernization is *differentiation*. While it is not a very colorful or suggestive term, the process it describes is dramatic. One feature of modern differentiation is *secularization*, the process through which various dimensions of life, such as politics, art, philosophy, and education, became freed from ecclesiastical control. One of the reasons the United States is rightly called the most fully modern nation is the great degree to which it has carried out the differentiation between religion and politics. While this "separation of church and state" has had great benefits for both religious and political life, it has also contained obvious dangers (which conservatives or traditionalists warned against from the beginning). One of these dangers is that politics would become wholly divorced from all moral principles (beyond self-interest). This possibility was foreshadowed in Machievelli and Hobbes, who are thereby generally seen as the first modern political philosophers. This possibility was widely realized in political theory in the late nineteenth and early twentieth centuries in the doctrine of realistic politics (*Realpolitik*), or power politics (*Machtpolitik*), based on the development, summarized in the previous section, of the notion that no rational basis exists for deciding upon ultimate values. Max Weber, who described this implication of the "disenchantment of the world," was himself a strong advocate of power politics on behalf of *his* ultimate value-decision, German nationalism,[28] and Weber's philosophy became widely influential in the United States through Hans Morgenau.[29] This type of political philosophy was carried out in Nazism and Stalinism, and long-standing just-war principles were violated by the American bombings of Tokyo, Hiroshima, and Nagasaki, and by American practices in Vietnam.[30]

The second process of differentiation most crucial for modernity was the separation of the economic realm from the political, which is central to the definitions of *liberalism* as a political philosophy and of *capitalism* as an economic philosophy, both of which are thought by many interpreters to lie at the heart of modernity. This separation meant the emancipation of economics from morality (that is, insofar as political power itself was still somewhat shaped by moral considerations), because an autonomous market would be guided only by the self-interest of the various actors.

How could this twofold emancipation of economic life from politics and morality, which was unheard of in the history of human society, have become possible? While the answer to this question is complex, part of the answer is that this emancipation was given an ideological justification. This ideology is called *economics*.[31] To justify the freedom of economics from political control, "the economy," which is an abstraction from the full reality of society, had to be portrayed as a distinct realm with inner consistency. Self-regulating "laws" of the marketplace, which can be discerned by the social scientist, had to exist.[32] To justify the separation from morality, modernity needed an argument that these laws would work for the general good, even though the dynamics of the market were fueled by avarice, which traditionally had been considered the most deadly of the sins. The argument modernity provided to meet this need was mentioned earlier: the marketplace works as if an "invisible hand" guided the process so that private vices produce public benefits.[33]

Through this "new theology" of the universal beneficence of profits, as Karl Polanyi calls it, a blanket moral pardon, as Robert Heilbroner says, was placed over the marketplace.[34] Philosophers of economics, from Adam Smith to the present day, including both defenders and critics alike, have listed the disastrous consequences of capitalism, for example, in diminishing the character of people, in destroying community, in fostering imperialism, and in producing massive disparities between rich and poor.[35] A few of these economic thinkers, especially Herman Daly, include on this list the destruction of the natural environment.[36] All these "side effects" have nevertheless been justified in terms of the original argument, that is, that the ability of capitalism to produce public good, now largely identified with economic wealth, more than compensates for its inevitable evils.[37] Those who do not accept this argument are generally called socialists.

The mention of socialism brings up a second argument that has been given from the outset of modernity for the separation of the economic from the political realm. This is the argument, strongly revived by antisocialist defenders of capitalism in our day, that this separation is necessary for a democratic system of government with political freedoms.[38] History shows, and critics of capitalism emphasize, that no necessary connection exists between capitalism and genuine political freedom: there have been many tyrannical nation-states that have participated fully in the capitalistic world order.[39] But even some strong critics of capitalism agree that the separation of the economic and political realms seems to be a necessary condition for political freedom.[40] Defenders of democratic socialism as an ideal can, of course, argue that no enduring examples of socialist democracy exist because each attempt to institute such a system, as in Czechoslovakia and Chile, was overthrown by hostile powers.

In any case, the political aspect of the modern ideology justifying the autonomy of the economic from the political realm is called *liberalism*. As Robert Heilbroner puts it, liberalism is the part of the modern ideology that explains the role of government in a society that has legitimated accumulation.[41] Liberalism in this sense is a matter of degree, the degree depending upon how strongly it is believed that government should abstain from "interference" in the marketplace. (The very term *interference* reflects the assumption that the economy is an autonomous realm which should, as much as possible, be left to run according to its own "laws.") Because the United States was founded as the liberal society *par excellence*, those who are called "conservatives" here are those who want to return to a purer form of liberalism, which means a purer form of modernism.[42]

Does this mean that a transition to socialism would be a move away from modernity? That might be the case in some respects if one meant the type of socialism that was represented in the thought of some pre-Marxist socialists and in some of Marx's own early writings, which Marx later derided as "utopian socialism."[43] Even Marxist "scientific" socialism is nonmodern in one respect, insofar as it rejects the differentiation of the economic from the political realm.

In several other respects, however, Marxism has generally been even more modernizing than capitalist liberalism. Although it has held out the promise of overcoming isolating individualism by restoring real community, which has probably constituted much of its appeal,[44] it has usually pursued this goal by aggressively working to eliminate as "irrational," "feudal," and "superstitious" all those traditional communities that stood between the individual and the centralized state economy.[45] In this context, the reunion of the political and economic realms can be regarded as even more modern than liberal differentiation, because it involves greater centralization and rationalization (as Joe Holland points out herein). Marxist socialism has thus perhaps effected modern dichotomization even more rapidly than have capitalist societies. If we take this dichotomization, along with industrialization, urbanization, technologization, bureaucratization, scientism, instrumental rationalization, secularization, egalitarianism, and materialism as the hallmarks of the modern, then industrial socialism has been more fully modern than industrial liberal capitalism.

In fact, Robert Nisbet said that Marxist socialism is in structure "simply capitalism minus private property."[46] That is a deliberately provocative remark, of course, because for Marx private property was of the essence of capitalism and lay at the root of all modern discontents. What Nisbet's quip reflects is the view of Max Weber and many others that capitalism with its private property is simply one of several manifestations of the larger process of modernization, many of whose features are problematic if not demonic.[47] Marx's rather single-minded focus on the evils of capitalism led him to discount other dangers and to assume that the elimination of the system of private property would by itself bring about a community of plenty, justice, and equality.[48]

Besides dichotomization and differentiation, with all of their variants, a third major feature of modern society is *mechanization*. Industrialization and technologization, of course, represent the process in which machines became central to society. Beyond this literal mechanization of life, a tendency has existed to make human society itself run as much like an efficient machine as possible. The modern division of labor is one chief example, along with the closely related phenomenon of "componentiality," in which each worker is an interchangeable component in the industrial machine.[49] The emergence of bureaucracies — which Weber called *animated machines*—is another. For Weber, the "bureaucratization" of modern society, which he regarded as the most insidious manifestation of modern "rationalization" (and one that would be even more fully developed in industrial socialist societies than in capitalist societies), was the chief threat of the modern age.[50] In Robert Heilbroner's view, the "imperatives" of industrial civilization, both in capitalist and socialist societies, have led to "the organization of work, of life, even of thought, in ways that accommodate men to machines rather than the much more difficult alternative."[51]

One more way to characterize modern society is in terms of its *materialism*, or what can be called its *economism*. This feature involves the assumption that, in the words of Louis Dumont, "the relations between men and things—material needs—are primary, the relations between men—society—secondary." Dumont goes on to say: "The primacy of the relations to things over the relations between men . . . is the decisive shift that distinguishes the modern civilization from all others and that corresponds to the primacy of the economic view in our ideological universe."[52] This means that society is subordinated to the economy, rather than vice versa.[53] In this new universe, the moral point of view has been replaced by the economic. This perspective "focuses on gain, wealth, material prosperity, as the core of social life."[54]

A second assumption of this materialistic or economistic view is reflected in the doctrine of the human being as *homo oeconomicus*. When human beings are viewed under this abstraction, the desire to better one's material condition indefinitely is regarded as inherent to human nature.[55] Also, insofar as modern human beings do have this desire, this abstraction from their full reality is treated as if it were the most important, virtually all-determining, feature of their existence. For Dumont, these first two features of the economistic point of view are closely connected with modern individualism: "society resolves itself into economics because only Individuals, that is, men stripped of all social characters, are considered."[56]

A third feature of this materialistic view was a creed, which according to Karl Polanyi underlay the Industrial Revolution, "a revolution as extreme and radical as ever inflamed the minds of sectarians." This was the materialistic creed "that all human problems could be resolved given an unlimited amount of material commodities."[57] This creed, combined with the treatment in public discourse of the human being as *homo oeconomicus*, has allowed us to assume a virtual identity between material prosperity and the general health and welfare of the society.[58] In crudest terms, the gross national product becomes *the* indicator of how well we are doing as a society. We can make this equation only, as Dumont sees it, insofar as there has been a divorce between our religion and our general values,[59] or, as Polanyi sees it, insofar as modernity has in effect adopted a new religion. Of the nineteenth century, Polanyi says: "A new way of life spread over the planet with a claim to universality unparalleled since the age when Christianity started out on its career, only this time the movement was on a purely material level."[60]

These several characterizations—in terms of dichotomization, differentiation, mechanization, and materialism—represent different angles on this extremely complex and unique social phenomenon we call *modernity*. While any one of them, or even any of their variants, may be lifted up as *the* driving force of modernity from which the others follow, it seems to me that each of them captures a central facet of modernity. Modernity can best be regarded as a pluralistic phenomenon involving the interaction of all these features (and some others not emphasized here, such as democracy, egalitarianism, and professionalism).

I do, however, accept the postmodern view that a certain priority belongs to the ideational and valuational elements. This view differs from the modern perspective, which regards beliefs and values primarily as derivative from social, especially economic, interests and practices. Analyses based on this modern assumption have taught us much about ourselves that should not be lost; that is, we should not react to materialism by returning to a premodern idealism, in which the power of material factors is ignored or belittled. But material interests and social practices can be given their due within a perspective that gives primacy to beliefs and values.

The difference between these two perspectives has a practical implication of first importance. Those modern perspectives that give priority to social practices and material factors, such as the economic system or a supposedly autonomous technology, provide no hope for overcoming the destructive trajectory of modernity short of violent revolution, which in our world would most likely be more destructive, and more immediately so, than the modernity it was seeking to derail. By contrast, a postmodern perspective offers the more hopeful vision that, through the emergence of a new worldview and a concomitant spirituality, with new interests, new values, new approaches, and new practices, the course of our world can be radically changed without cataclysmic revolution. This approach is always in danger, of course, of settling for the "Disneyland postmodernism" criticized by Richard Falk herein. But belief in the possibility of significant change without violent revolution need not mean naiveté, as Falk illustrates.

I turn now to a brief look at the postmodern spirituality that seems to be emerging in our time and then at some of the ideas for a postmodern social order.

III. POSTMODERN SPIRITUALITY

Given the centrality of individualism for modern spirituality and society, it is not surprising that no feature of postmodern spirituality is emphasized more than the reality of internal relations (see especially the essays by Catherine Keller and John Cobb herein). In contrast with the modern view, according to which relations to other people and things are regarded as external, "accidental," and derivative, postmodern authors portray relations as internal, essential, and constitutive. An individual does not first exist as a self-contained entity with various qualities on the basis of which he or she then has superficial interactions with other beings which do not affect his or her essence. The relations one has with one's body, one's larger natural environment, one's family, and one's culture are instead *constitutive* of one's very identity. The assumption that people growing up in a city will be essentially the same as their grandparents who lived on a farm is therefore completely unfounded. So is the assumption that people who have been "liberated" from traditional religious and civic communities will retain the positive characteristics of their grandparents while shedding only those characteristics associated with the restrictions of these communities.

A second feature of postmodern spirituality is its organicism, through which it simultaneously transcends modern dualism and modern materialism. Unlike dualistic moderns, postmodern persons do not feel like aliens in a hostile or indifferent nature. Rather, they feel at home in the world (as Charlene Spretnak stresses), and feel a sense of kinship with other species, which are viewed as having their own experiences, values, and purposes. Through this sense of at-homeness and kinship, the modern desire to master and possess is replaced in postmodern spirituality with a joy in communion and a desire for letting-be.

At the same time, this postmodern sense of oneness with nature is very different from that of materialistic modernity, in which oneness means a deterministic, relativistic reductionism. Because some degree of purposive freedom is ascribed to individuals at all levels of nature, the recognition that the human mind or soul is fully natural does not imply the illusory character of its apparent freedom. Postmodern spirituality recognizes that human beings have an extraordinary capacity for self-determination—which can be used for good or for ill. Because different levels of value-experience are seen throughout nature, the denial that human beings are the "lords of creation" for whose use the remainder was intended does not imply that a human being is of no more intrinsic value than a gnat. The postmodern vision thereby induces a spirituality in which ecological concern is combined with special concern for human welfare.

Because of this organicism, in which the self is felt to be analogous to other individuals throughout nature, it is natural for postmodern writers to find support for their self-understanding in postmodern science. For example, while modern spirituality was based upon an atomistic physics in which nature's ultimate constituents were only externally related to their environments, advocates of postmodern spirituality (such as John Cobb, Frederick Ferré, and Catherine Keller herein) point to ecology and quantum physics to undergird the sense that we are social beings, constituted by internal relations, through and through. Likewise, the generalization of self-determination to individuals at all levels is used to support the conviction that we are not *simply* social beings who are the products of our societies, but that we are genuinely creative beings who to some extent freely respond to the situations in which we find ourselves. The points to be made below, about the incorporation of the past, the future, divinity, and ethical and aesthetic norms, are also rooted in the "reenchantment of science" to which the first volume of this series was devoted.

Postmodern spirituality also has a new relation to time, that is, to the past and the future. As we saw, the radical individualism of modernity, which at first loosed people from the past in the name of the new and the future, has in the end undermined their concern for the future as well, leaving them with a literally *self*-defeating absorption in the present. Without returning to a premodern traditionalism in which the early modern orientation to novelty and the future are lost, postmodern spirituality recovers the concern and respect for the past. In recognizing that we are internally constituted by our relations, postmodern spirituality does not limit this recognition to our relations with contemporary objects. The present moment of experience is seen to enfold within itself, in some respect and to some degree, the entire past. Every individual, in fact, *is* its enfoldment of the past and its present reaction thereto. In other language—the language of Rupert Sheldrake in the first volume—we embody many long-standing "habits." What we call electrons, atoms, molecules, macromolecules, cells, and the human mind are habits of being that have endured for various lengths of time. This vision leads to an interest in the past, because knowledge of the past is essential to self-knowledge.

This vision also leads to a new conservatism, because it instills a new respect for ways of being and relating that have worked in the past. For example, the recognition that our bodies are composed of organisms that were formed over millions and even billions of years makes us wary of assuming that we can suddenly adjust to unique elements in our air, water, and food without suffering from unique epidemics; this type of conservatism fosters conservation. The idea that the human psyche embodies not only influences from its body but also the repeated experiences of past psyches (which is how Jung at least sometimes explained his "archetypes") leads us to be wary of assuming that we can adopt radically new forms of being human without suffering severe, perhaps terminal, psychic distress. Good reason therefore exists to suspect that the modern attempt to live without religious convictions and practices, and without the support of intimate communities, will not produce a sustainable society.

This renewed respect for tradition leads not, however, to a traditionalism in which novelty is shunned in principle, but to a transformative traditionalism. While recognizing that human nature is not infinitely plastic, postmodern spirituality sees that it is more malleable than the nature of other creatures. It recognizes, furthermore, that some of the changes introduced by modernity are good, a recognition embodied in the self-designation as *post*modern (rather than *pre*modern). Finally, postmodern spirituality regards some forms of possible novelty as calls forward from the divine reality, so that a pure conservatism would be a rejection of divine promptings. A central challenge for postmodern spirituality is to learn better to differentiate creative from destructive novelty.

Postmodern spirituality also contains a basis for interest in the future. The radical individualism of modernity allowed it to provide no such basis. Because the future was not thought to be internally related to the present, an individual's rational "self-interest" was assumed not to extend beyond his or her own lifetime. For example, when one of the best of our modern thinkers asks why we should act to affect events that will occur seventy-five years after our death (and hence after the deaths of our children and grandchildren), he says: "There is no rational answer."[61] The future is *not*, postmodern thought agrees, internally related to the present *in exactly the same way* as the past is; such a view, implying that the future is as settled as the past, would deny freedom. But, it *is* constitutive of the present that there will *be* a future, and indeed a future that grows out of the present and incorporates its contributions. The threat to the meaningfulness of human life induced by the possibility that we would have no posterity, thanks to the imminent nuclear annihilation of the human race, reveals how much the anticipation of the future is constitutive of present existence. Once we recognize this fact, we can see that action to protect the planet one hundred or one thousand years from now is as "rational" as action to provide money for our old age.

Another basis exists in postmodern spirituality for interest in the future, which is that we are internally constituted by our relationship to divinity. We care about the future of the world because we care about the everlasting divine reality.

The topic of the relation of the human being to divinity leads us to the heart of postmodern spirituality. Just as it rejects both dualism and materialism, postmodern spirituality rejects both supernaturalism and atheism. Although different constructive postmodernists describe it with different nuances, most of them affirm a vision that can be called *naturalistic panentheism*, according to which the world is present in deity and deity is present in the world. The shape of the world in this view results neither from the unilateral activity of deity nor from that of the creatures but from their cocreativity. As Richard Falk says, this vision portrays a dispersion of spiritual energy throughout the universe.

The recovery of a sacred creativity overcomes the debilitating nihilism of late modernity, including deconstructive postmodernity, without returning to the supernaturalism of early modernity, which so often fostered arrogance and complacency. The naturalism of this postmodern vision implies that the divine reality does not unilaterally and hence infallibly implant norms and beliefs into any one tradition. Nor can the divine reality be unilaterally expected to save the planet from the natural consequences of our foolish ways.

Although the divine reality does not unilaterally implant norms in human minds, these minds nevertheless can directly (if vaguely) experience divinely rooted norms. By recovering a vision of deity in which norms and values can have a natural abode, and by affirming a nonsensory level of perception through which such norms can be perceived, postmodern spirituality overcomes that complete relativism which followed from modernity's disenchantment of the world. This direct perception or intuition of norms does not obviate the necessity for aesthetic and ethical debate, because the perceptions are vague and often incompatible, and the conscious formulation of the perceived norms is always culturally conditioned. The point is that this direct perception of norms and values makes it *possible* for there to be genuine debate, for there to be rational, cognitive discussion about ethical and aesthetic judgments. The importance of this point cannot be overestimated, because it reverses the fateful opinion of Max Weber and other positivists that rational discussion about values or ends is impossible.

I conclude this overview of postmodern spirituality by noting one final feature, which is that it can be described, as many of the authors in this volume stress, as a postpatriarchal vision. This dimension of postmodern spirituality opens up the tantalizing possibility, mentioned especially by Richard Falk, Joe Holland, Catherine Keller, and Charlene Spretnak, that the transition before us could be even more momentous than overcoming the dominant movement of the past several hundred years. If modernity has been the extreme exemplification of patriarchal culture, so that the horrors of modernity have awakened the human psyche to the horrors implied by patriarchy, the transcendence of modern spirituality may also entail the transcendence of patriarchal spirituality, and hence of the dominant trajectory of the past several *thousand* years. We could be living through, in Falk's language, the first phase of a new axial breakthrough. Of course, cynics will dismiss these ideas as predictable end-of-the-century fantasies made doubly utopian by end-of-the-millennium expectations. But it belongs to postmodern spirituality to the postcynical. Change for the better *can* occur, and it is most likely to occur through people who are as far removed from cynicism as they are from utopianism.

IV. POSTMODERN SOCIETY

Postmodern thinking about society, in particular about social policy, including global policy, is relatively undeveloped. Philosophers, theologians, and natural scientists have been developing a postmodern worldview for about a century, with some even earlier anticipations. But serious, sustained thinking about the human social order from a postmodern perspective has begun only recently. Here too, of course, earlier anticipations exist which can be drawn upon by contemporary thinkers. But, for the most part, a postmodern approach to economics, politics, agriculture, science policy, technology, gender, global order, education, and other questions of social policy is in its infancy. *The* postmodern position on any of these issues does not exist. Therefore, I will not attempt to portray a consensus about what a postmodern society, and more generally a postmodern world, would be like. I will limit myself to a few comments about the issues raised earlier in the discussion of modern society, suggesting the general direction implied by postmodern spirituality or that being taken by some postmodern social theorists.

The stress on internal relations leads postmodern thinkers to want to overcome social individualism, or what I earlier called dichotomization, in which the naked individual and the nation-state with its economy are the two foci. Postmodern thought is communal or communitarian, stressing that social policy should be directed toward the preservation and re-creation of various forms of local community. This stress aligns postmodernism to some extent with neoconservatism, which has advocated public policy to preserve the mediating institutions described earlier.

Several differences exist between postmodernism and neoconservatism, however, even on this issue. First, neoconservatives focus primarily on family and church,[62] whereas postmodernists also support other forms of local community, such as bioregions and cultural regions. Second, neoconservatives support mediating institutions in large part to prop up the present megastructures, especially the capitalist economy and the system of nation-states, with its military arrangements.[63] Postmodern thinkers, such as John Cobb, Richard Falk, and Charlene Spretnak, characteristically oppose the present global economic order, and believe that the importance of the nation-state should be greatly reduced, in that some of its present functions should be allocated to smaller regions and others to a global authority. Third, neoconservatives seem to see strong religious belief in somewhat the same way Marx did (although with an opposite valuation), that is, as a basis for keeping people content with economic inequality.[64] Postmodern thinkers by contrast are interested in moving towards greater equality, both within each society and between societies, and regard religion as a potential source of support for this move. Finally, in advocating public policy to support religion, neoconservatives usually mean only Judaism and Christianity.[65] Postmodernists characteristically welcome a religiously pluralistic society. They hope that the various traditional religions will recognize their commonalities and also mutually transform themselves by appropriating truths and values from each others' particularities.

A second major theme of postmodern social thinkers is that public life must reflect religious values if there is to be a healthy and sustainable society. This conviction presupposes the prior convictions that public policy must reflect moral values, and that morality is ultimately rooted in a religious vision, which means a rejection of the modern assumption that morality can be autonomous.

Similarities and differences with neoconservatives are again evident.[66] Most of the differences probably flow out of the point mentioned above, that neoconservatives take "religion" in this context to mean "the Judeo-Christian heritage" while postmodernists have a more pluralistic view. In any case, the issue of "religion and politics" surely presents postmodern social theorists with one of their most important and difficult challenges. On the one hand, a widespread conviction exists, especially in the United States, that the "separation of church and state" is one of the essential pillars of freedoms we would not want to lose, both religious and political. On the other hand, a growing conviction exists, evidenced by the rise of neoconservatives and political evangelicals in this country and by various religious-political revivals in other countries, that a purely secular state is unsatisfactory and finally unsustainable. I hope this series can be a forum for postmodern explorations of this topic.

At least equally difficult is the question of economics in a postmodern world. On the one hand, a strong case can be made, as mentioned earlier, for the position that at least some autonomy of the economic realm *vis-à-vis* the political realm is a necessary condition for political and therefore even religious freedom. On the other hand, this separation has encouraged all sorts of disastrous consequences, both within individual societies and on a global scale, and seems to prevent us from taking effective action to reverse them.

To people with postmodern sensibilities, neither the present capitalist system nor some form of Marxist socialism, in the name of which capitalism is usually challenged, is acceptable. Postmodernists and neoconservatives agree that Marxist socialism embodies an even more extreme form of modernism than does the tradition of liberal capitalism.[67] However, neoconservatives, assuming that modern socialism and capitalism constitute the only real options, conclude from the weaknesses of Marxist socialism that we should reaffirm liberal capitalism with renewed zeal.[68] Postmodernists, by contrast, support the search for another alternative. The growing realization, which this series hopes to promote, that capitalism and socialism as we have known them) were *both* conceived and developed on the basis of *modern* presuppositions, by people with *modern* sensibilities, should help liberate our imaginations to come up with genuinely new possibilities.

In this regard, I should stress that Herman Daly herein restricts himself to the question of what steps could be taken immediately within capitalist economies to alleviate some of their most destructive effects. He does not address the larger question of what kind of economic order is implied by the postmodern vision and required for a truly postmodern world. His central point, however, that we must move to a steady-state economy (in his sense of this term), will surely be central to all postmodern proposals. This issue may be the basic one on which postmoderns and neoconservatives differ.[69]

Another general feature of postmodern social thought, given its emphases on internal relations, organicism, and creativity, is that it will seek to overcome the ways in which society has been mechanized in the modern period. For example, as Dean Freudenberger's essay stresses, agriculture must become less mechanistic, more organic, if it is to be sustainable. Also, the first priority will no longer be to have a team of laborers work as efficiently as a machine, with no concern for their need to exercise their own imagination and creativity and to participate in the decisionmaking process.

This feature will be supported by the final feature of postmodern social thinking to be mentioned here, which is that it rejects the materialism underlying modern social policy, along with the policy of indefinite growth which this materialistic creed promoted. Once we have returned the economic dimension of society to its normal place (that is, the place it has had in every human society except our aberrant modern one, in which it became the centerpiece and in effect the religion), it will no longer seem self-evident that machine-like efficiency should be more important during working hours than human-like enjoyment.

The end of the materialist era will also bring other benefits. For instance, once money and material goods no longer constitute our religion, and economic wealth is no longer a sufficient condition for social status, and once we have begun to live in terms of the realization that economic wealth, beyond a certain level, does not bring increased happiness, it will become much more possible to move toward global equity, in which all people have at least that minimal economic security necessary for a healthy and creative life. Also, as Daly intimates, once we have overcome the materialistic creed, we will no longer congratulate ourselves on the basis of how much of the planet we destroyed during the past year!

Most of the focus here has been on the ways in which the postmodern world must overcome destructive features of modernity; but there were also many good features of modernity which it is the task of postmodernity to continue and extend. Among these were the ideal of progress and the trinitarian ideal of "liberty, equality, and fraternity" lifted up by the French Revolution. Having discussed fraternity already under the heading of "community," I will look at liberty and equality and then the ideal of progress.

Modernity has regarded liberty and equality as "trade-offs": the more we have of one, it is thought, the less we can have of the other. These two ideals have accordingly been championed one-sidedly by modernity's two political-economic systems, with capitalist democracy emphasizing liberty to the relative neglect of equality, and Marxist socialism emphasizing equality to the relative neglect of liberty.

The liberty granted by modern capitalist democracy at its best is an unprecedented achievement. While some aspects of this freedom must be curtailed if we are to survive (such as the freedom to reproduce, consume and pollute without limit), many aspects of it should be preserved and even extended in a postmodern world. Examples are the freedom to read, to speak, to assemble, to worship, to publish, to advance, to move about, to privacy, and to due process. No longing for forms of community and equality incompatible with these freedoms, and no criticisms of modern democracy's failures with respect to realizing these freedoms, should lead us to abandon them as ideals.

The realization of these ideals has indeed been limited. The capitalist world has not in practice been the champion of universal freedom, but has undermined the economic and political liberties of many in the name of the unbridled economic freedom of a few. While most of the First World capitalist nations have encouraged democracy at home, they have actively worked against the development of democratic self-rule in Third World countries upon whom inequitable economic agreements have been imposed.[70] Even within these First World countries, the economic liberty of capitalists has meant the denial of freedom to others, as exemplified by the treatment of Blacks in the United States and South Africa. Political freedom and freedom of the press are also much more restricted within capitalist democracies than may appear at first sight: citizens are generally free to vote only for candidates acceptable to the wealthy, and most of the news media are controlled by this same class. Even if the control of politics and the mainline press by a capitalist class is less complete than it is portrayed to be by socialist critics,[71] this control is much greater than acknowledged by the mainline press. In sum, while the freedoms realized in capitalist democracies are real, they fall short of the publically proclaimed ideals, largely because the first freedom is the freedom of the wealthy to protect and increase their wealth.

Capitalist democracy has fared as poorly with the ideal of equality as with that of community. It has, to be sure, promoted equalitarianism in some respects, especially with regard to aesthetic and cultural taste. Indeed, Toqueville, who regarded equality as the central ideal of the modern age, saw it as being embodied most fully in the United States.[72] But the capitalist world order has brought about unprecedented gaps between rich and poor—both between the richest and the poorest within each nation, and between the richest and the poorest nations. Because status and power are primarily functions of money in a capitalist society, furthermore, the great inequalities of wealth mean great inequalities in almost every other dimension of life as well, including that much vaunted dimension called "opportunity." Nothing approaching equality of opportunity is possible in conjunction with gross inequalities of wealth, status, and power.

Modern socialism has sought to create societies in which the inequalities characteristic of capitalist societies are greatly reduced. The fact that full equality has not been realized should not blind us to the fact that the gap between the richest and the poorest 10 percent in socialist societies is much less than it is in capitalist societies. This movement toward equality should be endorsed and extended in a postmodern world.

The chief failure of socialist nations has been their failure to take seriously the need to build in safeguards for freedom from the abuse of political power.[73] More than not taking this need seriously, socialists in power have generally regarded liberty as incompatible with the main goal of combining equality with economic progress.

The idea of moving forward to a postmodern world, rather than seeking escape from the horrors of modernity through a return to a premodern form of life, means incorporating the virtues of modernity as well as overcoming its vices. Among the virtues are these ideals of community, liberty, and equality. Because of modernity's individualism—its denial of our internal relatedness to the past, the land, and each other—it has destroyed community more than it has promoted it. As discussed earlier, community has been seen as antithetical to both freedom and progress. The modern world has done much better with liberty and equality, but not in combination, because each was understood so as to seem largely antithetical to the other. This understanding also seems to be due to modernity's individualism. The postmodern sensibility, with its recognition of internal relations, does not regard liberty, equality, and community as in tension with each other, so that we must live with "trade-offs" between each pair, but as mutually supportive. For example, no genuine, enduring community can exist without liberty and equality (in some significant sense), and no genuine and enduring liberty can exist without community and equality. The postmodern social imagination may hence find a way to champion all three equally.

But what about the ideal of progress? Has it not been one of those modern ideals that has been proven false? The answer to this question depends upon what one means by "the myth of progress." Does it mean the assumption that a culture that rejects most of the past as superstition and devotes itself to increased material comfort through the technological domination of nature will bring about a world of peace, freedom, happiness, and moral excellence? If so, then the ideal of progress has been proved to be a myth in the derogatory sense of the term. But if we ask, "Did the modern world make progress in those areas to which it devoted itself wholeheartedly?" then the answer must be a resounding "Yes." Modern spirituality has made progress in at least three areas that would astound a sixteenth-century figure such as John Calvin if he could return to see it. These areas are (1) the understanding of nature, especially those aspects of nature that lend themselves to mechanistic, reductionistic, quantifiable approaches—we can imagine Calvin's amazement at modern astrophysics or explanations of heredity based on DNA research; (2) the technological domination of nature, especially after technology was wedded to modern physics and chemistry—we can imagine Calvin's amazement at our trips to the moon, and our vaccinations to prevent scarlet fever; and (3) the economic enrichment of a portion of the people—we can imagine Calvin's amazement at the wealth of the richest 5 percent of the world (and especially at hearing the theory that *he* was responsible for it).[74]

This record of success shows what the human spirit can do when it becomes religiously committed to a goal. Imagine what we could do if we became religiously committed to a human society of liberty, equality, and community, with "community" understood as the whole biotic community. The possibilities are beyond imagination, because we would be employing all the scientific and technological knowledge garnered during the modern period for postmodern purposes, and therefore for the long-term good of the planet as a whole. This means that we would have a postmodern politics, a postmodern social policy, a postmodern economics, a postmodern agriculture, and a postmodern technology, as described by the authors herein.

I conclude by repeating that the essays in this volume, including this introductory essay, are not intended as definitive statements of *the* position of this form of postmodernism on any issue. They are first proposals, presented to stimulate thinking, conversation, action to begin testing them in practice—and also further proposals. This series is, in fact, open to unsolicited essays presenting alternative postmodern proposals on any of the topics discussed herein, as well as other topics relevant to a postmodern world, such as architecture, art, business, criminology, education, mass media, medical policy, political leadership, spiritual discipline, transportation, and urban life. Let us see if we cannot come up with a better way to organize our portion of the world!

NOTES

1. See B. F. Skinner, *Beyond Freedom and Dignity* (New York: Bantam/Vintage, 1972).

2. See John Cobb and Catherine Keller in this volume; Louis Dumont, *From Mandeville to Marx: The Genesis and Triumph of Economic Ideology* (Chicago: University of Chicago Press, 1977), 4, 55–59, 76, 106–07, 113; Robert Nisbet, *The Sociological Tradition* (New York: Basic Books, 1966), 8, 47, 49, 59, 272, 300; Karl Polanyi, *The Great Transformation* (Boston: Beacon Press, 1957), 85, 103, 258; Peter Berger, *Facing Up to Modernity: Excursions in Society, Politics, and Religion* (New York: Basic Books, 1977), 60–61, 71–72; David Riesman, *Individualism Reconsidered and Other Essays* (New York: Free Press, 1954), 26; and Robert N. Bellah *et al., Habits of the Heart: Individualism and Commitment in American Life* (Berkeley: University of California Press, 1985), *passim.*

3. See my essay herein. It is interesting to note Descartes' early modern view. He said that minds and bits of matter fit the definition of "substance" except in one respect: they do require God in order to exist. Only God, who was thought to be absolutely independent of everything else, was a full-fledged substance.

4. See Louis Dumont, *From Mandeville to Marx*, 7, 15.

5. See Sandra G. Harding, *The Science Question in Feminism* (Ithaca, N.Y.: Cornell University Press, 1986), 226.

6. See Karl Polanyi, *The Great Transformation*, 113–17, 163–65, 178.

7. See the discussion of dualism and its motives in the introduction to David Ray Griffin, ed., *The Reenchantment of Science: Postmodern Proposals* (Albany: State University of New York Press, 1988).

8. See Peter Berger's *Facing up to Modernity*, 73–74, from which I borrowed the term *futurism.*

9. See Stephen P. L. Turner and Regis A. Factor, *Max Weber and the Dispute over Reason and Value: A Study in Philosophy, Ethics, and Politics* (London: Routledge & Kegan Paul, 1984), 38, 65, 96, 97, 183. Weber says that "the fate of our times is characterized by rationalization and intellectualization and, above all, the 'disenchantment of the world' [so that] precisely the ultimate and most sublime values have retreated from public life" ("Science as Vocation," in H. H. Gerth and C. Wright Mills, eds., *From Max Weber* [New York: Oxford University Press, 1958], 155). Earlier in this essay Weber said that, because it is impossible for us to prove any value-judgments, the world is "ethically irrational" (122). (I am indebted for these references, and some in notes 11 and 12, to an unpublished paper by Kenneth Surin entitled "The Disenchantment of the World and Max Weber's 'Ethic of Responsibility'.")

10. Francis Hutcheson's theory that we were endowed with a "moral sense" by the "Author of Nature," and its influence on David Hume, Adam Smith, and Thomas Jefferson, are discussed by Garry Wills in *Inventing America: Jefferson's Declaration of Independence* (New York: Vintage Books, 1978), chap. 13, entitled " . . . endowed by their creator . . . ". Wills points out on page 193 that this theory enabled Hutcheson to circumvent the moral pessimism that would otherwise follow from the sensationist epistemology of Locke and Hume; the reference to the Author of Nature as the source of the moral sense is on page 205.

11. Nisbet, *The Sociological Tradition*, 141, 144, 256, 293–96. For the connection between this purely instrumental rationality and Weber's "ethic of responsibility," which is limited to means-ends relations, see Wolfgang Schluchter, "Value-Neutrality and the Ethics of Responsibility," in Schluchter and Guenther Roth, eds., *Max Weber's Vision of History: Ethics and Methods* (Berkeley: University of California Press, 1981).

12. Jürgen Habermas describes Weber's position as "decisionism" in "Value-Freedom and Objectivity" in Otto Stammer, ed., *Max Weber and Sociology Today* (Oxford: Blackwell, 1971), 64. See the discussion in Turner and Factor, *Max Weber and the Dispute over Reason and Value*, 50, 182.

13. Polanyi, *The Great Transformation*, 30, 249–50; Dumont, *From Mandeville to Marx*, 61; Irving Kristol, *Reflections of a Neoconservative* (New York: Basic Books, 1983), 155, 161, 180. On this topic, R. H. Tawney said: "To found a science of society upon the assumption that the appetite for economic gain is . . . to be accepted, like other natural forces . . . would have appeared to the medieval thinker as hardly less irrational or less immoral than to make the premise of social philosophy the unrestrained operation of such necessary human attributes as pugnacity or the sexual instinct" (*Religion and the Rise of Capitalism* [New York: Harcourt, Brace & World], 31, quoted in Robert L. Heilbroner, *The Making of Economic Society* [Englewood Cliffs, N. J.: Prentice-Hall, 1962], 44).

14. Dumont, *From Mandeville to Marx*, 61, 70; Robert L. Heilbroner, The *Nature and Logic of Capitalism* (New York: W. W. Norton, 1985), 110–16.

15. Dumont, *From Mandeville to Marx*, 62–70.

16. See Irving Kristol, *Reflections of a Neoconservative*, 50–51, 81, 175, 243, 250, 256, and Daniel Bell, *The Cultural Contradictions of Capitalism* (New York: Basic Books, 1976), 55, 84, 145, and esp. 86, where it is argued that "modernity itself produces an incoherence in culture."

17. See Christopher Lasch, *The Culture of Narcissism: American Life in an Age of Diminishing Expectations* (New York: W. W. Norton, 1979), xv, xvi, 3–7, 13, 22, 27, 28, 68–69, 210–11. Narcissism for Lasch is not the result of an inflated sense of self but of a *loss* of self and individuality (30, 37, 70, 210).

18. See *ibid.,* 27, 50, and Robert Jay Lifton, *The Broken Connection: On Death and the Continuity of Life* (New York: Simon and Schuster, 1979), or Lifton's portion of *Indefensible Weapons: The Political and Psychological Case Against Nuclearism* (New York: Basic Books, 1982), coauthored with Richard Falk.

19. This is Heidegger's interpretation of Nietzsche's proclamation that God is dead. See "The Word of Nietzsche: 'God is Dead'," in Martin Heidegger, *The Question Concerning Technology: Heidegger's Critique of the Modern Age,* William Lovett, trans. (New York: Harper & Row, 1977). Hans Jonas says that Heidegger's thought provides no norm by which to decide the way to answer the call of being, "no norm except depth, resolution, and the sheer force of being that issues the call." Jonas connects this lack in Heidegger's thought to the latter's notorious proclamation as rector of the University of Freiburg in 1933: "Not doctrines and 'ideas' be the rules of your being. The Führer himself and alone is the present and future German reality and its law. Learn ever deeper to know: that from now on each and every thing demands decision, and every action, responsibility. Heil Hitler!" (*The Phenomenon of Life: Toward a Philosopohical Biology* [New York: Harper & Row, 1966], 247 n. 11).

20. See Richard Hofstadter, *Social Darwinism in American Thought*, rev. ed. (Boston: Beacon Press, 1955), and John Kenneth Galbraith, *The Affluent Society* (New York: Mentor Books, 1958), 53–58.

21. See Evelyn Fox Keller, *Reflections on Gender and Science* (New Haven, Conn.: Yale University Press, 1985); Sandra G. Harding, *The Science Question in Feminism*; and Susan R. Bordo, *The Flight to Objectivity: Essays on Cartesianism & Culture* (Albany: State University of New York Press, 1987), esp. chap. 6, "The Cartesian Masculinization of Thought and the Seventeenth-Century Flight from the Feminine."

22. See Nisbet, *The Sociological Tradition,* 73–80, 141, and Berger, *Facing up to Modernity*, 120–21.

23. Berger, *Facing up to Modernity*, 122.

24. *Ibid.*, 133, 132.

25. *Ibid.*, 61.

26. Nisbet, *The Sociological Tradition,* 91–95, 300–04.

27. Lasch characterizes narcissism as the psychological dimension of the late modern individual's dependence "on the state, the corporation, and other bureaucracies" (*The Culture of Narcissism*, 10). He believes that personal dependence has been replaced not with Weber's "bureaucratic rationality" but with bureaucratic dependence (229).

28. See Turner and Factor, *Max Weber and the Dispute over Reason and Value*, 59, 63–64, 68, 75, 91.

29. *Ibid.*, 172, 178.

30. See Michael Waltzer, *Just and Unjust Wars: A Moral Argument with Historical Illustrations* (New York: Basic Books, 1977).

31. Heilbroner, *The Nature and Logic of Capitalism*, 111; Dumont, *From Mandeville to Marx*, 17, 25.

32. Dumont, *From Mandeville to Marx*, 33, 37.

33. *Ibid.*, 37–38, 61, 70, 75; Polanyi, *The Great Transformation*, 102.

34. Polanyi, *The Great Transformation*, 133, cf. 135; Heilbroner, *The Nature and Logic of Capitalism,* 116.

35. Heilbroner, *The Nature and Logic of Capitalism*, 108–118, 135–40, 157–58; Galbraith, *The Affluent Society*, 39–46; Kristol, *Confessions of a Neoconservative,* 41, 53, 117, 166–69, 173–75, 321.

36. Daly's concern is echoed by Heilbroner in *The Nature and Logic of Capitalism*, 135, and *An Inquiry into the Human Prospect: Updated and Reconsidered for the 1980s* (New York: W. W. Norton, 1980), 74, 98. In the light of the fact that industrial socialism has not been any less destructive of nature, it is interesting to note that Engels had pointed out capitalism's environmental destructiveness and hoped that socialism would involve a return to oneness with nature (Alvin W. Gouldner, *The Two Marxisms: Contradictions and Anomalies in the Development of Theory* [New York: Oxford University Press, 1980], 265).

37. For example, Thomas Schelling writes:

The free market may not do much, or anything, to distribute opportunities and resources among people the way you and I might like them distributed . . . ; it may encourage individualistic rather than group values. It may lead to asymmetrical personal relationships between employee and employer. . . . The market may even perform disastrously when inflation and depression are concerned. Still, within these serious limitations it does remarkably well in coordinating or harmonizing or integrating the effects of . . . individuals and organizations (*Micromotives and Macrobehavior* [New York: W. W. Norton, 1978], 23).

After quoting this passage, Robert Heilbroner comments: "the market is given its ultimate blessing on terms that excuse a maldistribution of opportunities and resources, unsocial values, unequal bargaining power, and perhaps 'disastrous' performance during inflation or depression. One is tempted to ask by what criteria the system would be deemed a failure" (*The Nature and Logic of Capitalism,* 115n–116n).

38. Milton Friedman, *Capitalism and Freedom* (Chicago: University of Chicago Press, 1962, 1982), 7–21; Kristol, *Confessions of a Neoconservative,* 41, 76, 167; Riesman, *Individualism Reconsidered,* 29.

39. Heilbroner, *The Nature and Logic of Capitalism*, 125–28. For support, Heilbroner cites Milton Friedman, who, while arguing that capitalism is "a necessary condition for political freedom," admits that it is "not a sufficient condition" (*Capitalism and Freedom*, 10), citing several examples, to which Heilbroner adds some more.

40. Heilbroner seems to accept this view (*ibid.*, 126–27).

41. *Ibid.*, 121–22.

42. That is at least what conservative liberalism means in theory. In practice, the difference between conservative and liberal liberalism concerns only the *kind* of political intervention into the marketplace with laws and public funds that is

favored, that is, whether it is to give direct aid to the capitalist participants in the process or to alleviate some of the "side effects" of the process, especially for the poorest members of the society.

43. See Gouldner, *The Two Marxisms*, 193–96; Kristol, *Confessions of a Neoconservative*, 116–20, 149.

44. See Berger, *Facing up to Modernity*, 59–60, 136.

45. Dumont, *From Mandeville to Marx*, 107–08, 113, 129–37, 147–48, 174; Nisbet, *The Sociological Tradition*, 25–26, 52, 69–70, 134; Robert Heilbroner, *Marxism: For and Against* (New York: W. W. Norton, 1980), 167, 170.

46. Nisbet, *The Sociological Tradition*, 58. Robert Heilbroner, whose perspective is far removed from Nisbet's, points out the great similarities between industrial capitalism and industrial socialism in terms of their effects (*Inquiry into the Human Prospect*, 93).

47. Nisbet, *The Sociological Tradition*, 145, 285–86, 293.

48. *Ibid.*, 137; Berger, *Facing up to Modernity*, 136.

49. The notion of "componentiality," as developed in Peter L. Berger, Brigitte Berger, and Hansfried Kellner, *The Homeless Mind: Modernization and Consciousness* (New York: Random House, 1973), 27–28, 33–35, 112, 182–83, is cited by Charlene Spretnak in this volume. The modern notion that workers are or should be "components" in a mechanical system implied that their creativity should be kept to a minimum. In his famous work, *The Philosophy of Manufacturers* (1835; Frank Cass, 1967), Andrew Ure said:

> [T]he more skillful the workman, the more self-willed and intractable he is apt to become, and, of course, the less fit a component of a mechanical system. . . . The grand object therefore of the modern manufacturer is, through the union of capital and science to reduce the task of his work-people to the exercise of vigilance and dexterity (20).

Ure's "great doctrine" was that "when capital enlists science in her service, the refractory hand of labour will always be taught docility" (368). These passages are quoted in Brian Easlea, *Witch Hunting, Magic and the New Philosophy: An Introduction to Debates of the Scientific Revolution 1450–1750* (Atlantic Highlands, N. J.: Humanities Press, 1980), 240–41.

50. See Nisbet, *The Sociological Tradition*, 145–48; Turner and Factor, *Max Weber and the Dispute over Reason and Value*, 79; and Max Weber, "Bureaucracy," in his *Economy and Society* (Los Angeles: University of California Press, 1978).

51. Heilbroner, *An Inquiry into the Human Prospect*, 94.

52. Dumont, *From Mandeville to Marx*, 81.

53. *Ibid.*, 33, 54, 59–60. Karl Polanyi says of modern society: "Instead of economy being embedded in social relations, social relations are embedded in the economic system" (*The Great Transformation*, 57). Some Marxists say that the political and cultural dimensions of society are totally determined, at least "in the

last analysis," by the economic dimension, which provides the substructure for the others. Other Marxists are more pluralistic. They allow some autonomy to the cultural and political spheres, insisting only that these spheres must be *consistent with* the economic relations and modes of production. Alvin Gouldner has shown that both positions can be found in the writings of Marx and Engels themselves (*The Two Marxisms*, 40, 47, 59, 82-87, 94-104, 199-220, 222-46, 300-04). Defenders of liberal capitalism follow Max Weber in being pluralistic, rejecting the substructure-super-structure analysis. While this pluralism avoids the reductionism of much Marxism, the vehement rejection of the Marxian analysis often results in a blindness to the great extent to which the economic realm, in terms of what Marxists call "the ruling class," does exert hegemony within capitalist societies. For example, Irving Kristol says that, "in a democracy, the people are the ruling class," and explicitly denies that big business manipulates the economic and political system (*Reflections of a Neoconservative*, 63, 205-07). Robert Heilbroner, who believes that we must speak of capitalists as the ruling class (*The Nature and Logic of Capitalism*, 129-32), says: "What the conservative view fails to recognize . . . is that power is rarely a wild card in the game of politics, but a trump suit held by the ruling interests of society" (*An Inquiry into the Human Prospect*, 147). Thorstein Veblen, certainly no Marxist, said around the turn of the century: "Nowhere else does the captain of big business rule the affairs of the nation, civil and political, and control the conditions of life so unreservedly, as in democratic America" (quoted in John P. Diggins, *The Bard of Savagery: Thorstein Veblen and Modern Social Theory* [New York: Seabury Press, 1978], 26).

54. Dumont, *From Mandeville to Marx*, 76.

55. Irving Kristol expresses this view, saying: "The overwhelming majority of men and women are naturally and incorrigibly interested in improving their material conditions" (*Reflections of a Neoconservative*, 193). Karl Polanyi, by contrast, argues that the tendency of human beings to seek to make a profit through exchanges had seldom been a significant feature of economic life prior to modern times (*The Great Transformation*, 43-55). Galbraith argues that most of the economic wants that are satisfied by modern production had been artificially created by the production process and its concomitant advertising. As he mentions, Lord Keynes himself distinguished between "absolute" and "relative" needs, saying that only the latter, through which people are led to feel superior to others, might be insatiable (*The Affluent Society*, 122). Galbraith further suggests that the desire to acquire more and better goods takes on a life of its own in modern society because this society "evaluates people by the products they possess." In other words: "The urge to consume is fathered by the value system . . . " (126). The position taken by Polanyi and Galbraith reflects their view that, beyond a certain level of material comfort and security, wealth is almost always valued not for its own sake but for the social status it brings. That is, relative wealth becomes more important than absolute wealth (Polanyi 47, 128, 153; Galbraith 122-123). Galbraith adds that economic wealth is much more important in the modern age than previously because modern society has eliminated many of the other traditional means of acquiring status (126). I would add that modern materialism gives economic success a religious significance that makes it personally satisfying even apart from social status.

56. Dumont, *From Mandeville to Marx*, 76.

57. Polanyi, *The Great Transformation*, 40.

58. Dumont, *From Mandeville to Marx*, 75.

59. *Ibid.*, 23.

60. Polanyi, *The Great Transformation*, 130.

61. Heilbroner, *An Inquiry into the Human Prospect*, 180.

62. See Kristol, *Reflections of a Neoconservative*, 77.

63. *Ibid.*, xiii, 58, 64, 76–77, 227, 228, 240, 242, 256, 277. Kristol believes that it is an illusion to think we are "moving toward an eventual 'world community'," and that the "very notion of a world without war is fantastic" (227, 320).

64. For Kristol's antagonism to programs for economic equality, see *ibid.*, xiv, 195, 200, 324. On this question, and that of the relation of religion thereto, see Peter Steinfels, *The Neoconservatives: The Men Who Are Changing America's Politics* (New York: Simon and Schuster, 1979), 52, 62, 107, 180, 182–83.

65. See Kristol, *op. cit.*, 41.

66. See *ibid.*, ix, 50–51, 57, 76, 124–26, 148–49.

67. See *ibid.*, 33–34, 80, 118–20.

68. See *ibid.*, 114, 118, 122.

69. For Irving Kristol, the assumption of continued economic growth is absolutely essential to the defense of capitalism; see *ibid.*, xii, 76, 89, and esp. 322, where he says: "Now, it is true that, if there is no economic growth . . . then the question of distribution becomes an overwhelming moral issue. In my opinion, it is a trivial moral issue in our world because economic growth solves the problem—the problem of poverty—toward which redistribution aims." Robert Heilbroner is one of the few major economists besides Daly to stress the importance of moving to a stationary economy (*An Inquiry into the Human Prospect*, 99–110). He points out that this move would mean facing "the explosive issue of income redistribution" (102). One major difference between Daly and Heilbroner is that the latter seems to assume that a steady-state economy would mean a "static society" (162–64), while Daly recognizes that a nongrowth economy allows many other types of growth to continue, such as "growth in grace."

70. See, for example, Walter Lefeber, *Inevitable Revolutions: The United States in Central America,* expanded ed. (New York: W. W. Norton, 1984); Edward S. Herman, *The* Real *Terror Network: Terrorism in Fact and Propaganda* (Boston: South End Press, 1982); Noam Chomsky, *Turning the Tide: U. S. Intervention in Central America and the Struggle for Peace* (Boston: South End Press, 1985); Kevin Danaher, *In Whose Interest? A Guide to U. S.–South Africa Relations* (Washington, D. C.: Institute for Policy Studies, 1984); Susan George, *How the Other Half Dies: The Real Reasons for World Hunger* (Totawa, N. J.: Rowman & Allanheld, 1977); and Richard J. Barnet, *Roots of War: The Men and Institutions Behind U. S. Foreign Policy* (1971; New York: Penguin Books, 1982).

71. See Michael Parenti, *Inventing Reality: The Politics of the Mass Media* (New York: St. Martin's Press, 1986).

72. Nisbet, *The Sociological Tradition*, 183–86.

73. On the failure of Marx and Marxism to take political freedom seriously and to build in safeguards to protect it against the autonomous (from economics) drive for political power, see Nisbet, *The Sociological Tradition*, 136, and Gouldner, *The Two Marxisms*, 54. Robert Heilbroner observes:

> The *Manifesto* has no aspirations or declarations with regard to political dissent, civil rights, social or sexual emancipation, or—above all—intellectual freedom. The main battlegrounds on which liberty has been defeated in socialist countries are thus not even identified as strategic territory by Marx and Engels. . . . Still today . . . Marxist thought is almost entirely indifferent to, or ignorant of, any systematic consideration of the means of containing political power'' (*Marxism*, 160, 165).

74. The reference is to the thesis of Max Weber (in *The Protestant Ethic and the Spirit of Capitalism*), later reformulated by R. H. Tawney (in *Religion and the Rise of Capitalism*), that Protestantism, in particular Calvinism, was a major factor in the rise of capitalism.

2

POSTMODERN DIRECTIONS

Charlene Spretnak

In the city across the bay from the town where I live stands an enormous monument to the values of modernity. It is a time capsule, presented in colorful murals, of bold expressions of industrial progress, of mastery over nature, of humans as *homo oeconomicus*. It is, in short, a paean to the materialist interpretation of human existence. Moreover, it proclaims the "individual-liberationist"[1] values of modern existence: people are either at work or moving through an urban street scene as atomized components. There are no churches, no First Communion or Bar Mitzvah celebrations, no community events, no ethnic societies. There are no families (except for a few mothers with young children and except for one hidden-away scene of a strangely linear and transparent wealthy family, suggesting perhaps a thin quality of emotional interactions among the rich). Everyone has been absorbed as individuals into mass culture, fed by mass media. Their lives have been shaped to serve "progress" and the needs of the nation-state with its demands for open-ended, unqualified economic growth.

Do these murals depict life in a capitalist or a socialist country? Ironically, the artists—who were mostly leftists and some of whom painted communist symbols into the murals—chose for the dominating figures across from the entrance the very same figures that loom over the entrance to the stock exchange, that temple of capitalism a few blocks away: the mighty industrial worker and the mighty agricultural worker.

The murals were commissioned by the federal Public Works of Art Project (PWAP) for the inside walls of the base of Coit Tower, a 180-foot-high, round shaft constructed in 1933 on Telegraph Hill in San Francisco. The following year, twenty-six artists (almost all male) and nineteen assistant artists (largely female) were hired to paint 3,691 square feet of murals depicting life in California. *Modern* life is what they painted, as might be expected.

Because it is increasingly apparent that modernity has failed to fulfill its promises of "a better life" in many of the deepest senses, the challenge of figuring out what went wrong has become a growth industry among intellectuals and political activists of the 1980s. Some of the most useful analytical tools I have encountered in my own research are the following concepts framed by the sociologists Peter Berger, Brigitte Berger, and Hansfried Kellner in *The Homeless Mind: Modernization and Consciousness.*[2] A number of the themes they discuss in connection with technological production also apply to the symbolic universe of modernity as a whole: functional rationalization (the imposition of rational controls over the material world, social relations, and the self); componentiality (the conception of reality as being composed of clearly separable components); multirelationality (dealing with an enormous variety of relations); makeability (a problem-solving approach to reality, which is apprehended as "makeable"); pluralization (the vastly intensified demands on human consciousness to shift among multiple realities or "life-worlds"); and progressivity (an "upward and onward" view of the world). While their terms are clunky or even ugly, a not infrequent attribute in the jargon of sociology, their analysis is a useful contribution to beyond-right-and-left approaches in contemporary thinking about postmodern possibilities.

Berger, Berger, and Kellner propose that humans living in a modern society are afflicted with a permanent identity crisis. Modern identity is open-ended, transitory, and liable to ongoing change, whereas a particular subjective realm of identity is the individual's main foothold in reality. They note that modern identity is "peculiarly individuated," such that the right to plan and fashion one's life as freely as possible is taken to be a basic right, elaborately legitimated by a variety of modern ideologies.

Such considerations inevitably lead these sociologists to religion, which they define as a cognitive and normative structure that makes it possible for people to "feel at home" in the universe. While they suggest no solutions, they observe that pluralization has a secularizing effect, weakening the hold of religion and pushing it into the realm of private life—or "privatizing" it, as they say. The compensations of the private sphere are generally experienced as being fragile, possibly artificial, and essentially unreliable. Hence, the task of each individual's creating a do-it-yourself universe in order to grasp at meaning is frought with frustration. We of the modern era are homeless in the cosmos.

What are the historic roots of our homelessness? In New Age or "new paradigm" circles, one often hears the explanation that our contemporary "mechanistic" worldview began with the Scientific Revolution of the sixteenth and seventeenth centuries with the aggressive, yet monstrously limited, empiricism of Descartes, Newton, and Bacon. Actually, we fell in with bad company long before that.

Archaeology—especially the pioneering work of R. Rachel Levy and Marija Gimbutas—has illuminated our heritage of a human consciousness rooted in cosmology. From the Upper Paleolithic through the Neolithic era in Europe, the excavated art, ritual objects, and womb-like caves reflect a variety of peoples who were clearly "at home" in the universe. Gimbutas's *Goddesses and Gods of Old Europe, 6500–3500 B.C.*[3] includes scores of photographs of sculptures that combine human form with symbols of the elements or animal forms, such as the Bird Goddess or the Snake Goddess, which were versions of the Great Mother Goddess who gave forth bountiful gifts on Her surface and received people back into her Earth-womb when they died. By far the most numerous human-like statues from the Neolithic era, from Spain to Siberia, are the ritually placed Goddess images, expressions of connectedness with the forces of birth, death, and regeneration. Archaeologists have found, as well, a wide range of ceramic pieces bearing symbols of the four directions, the mountains, the flowing water, the land—the sacred forms of this magnificent blue-green planet.

Earth-based spirituality honored the female for her elemental mysteries—bleeding in rhythm with the moon, swelling up like the full moon and pulling *people* from her womb, and transforming food into milk for the young. But the honoring of Mother Earth and her daughters was smashed when three waves of barbarian invaders, nomadic cow-herders, migrated from the Eurasian steppes into southeastern Europe, beginning in 4500 B.C. (They also moved down into India, the Middle East, and the Near East.) Prior to the invasions the settlements of the Old Europeans, with their sophisticated art and subtle awareness of cosmology, had been unfortified; additional evidence that they lived in peace is that no caches of weapons or concentrations of skeletons with battle-like wounds have ever been found in excavations of Old Europe. The Indo-European invaders were "indifferent to art," in the words of Professor Gimbutas, and had only two symbols, a sun and a pine tree, which they impressed with a primitive stamping technique. They introduced into Western culture the patriarchal chieftan system (previously the graves had been roughly egalitarian between the sexes), the cult of the sky-god, and adoration of the warrior, which are with us still.

Throughout centuries of European history, the struggle between the Old Religion—the revering of Mother Earth and Her mysteries—and the imposed sky-god religion was stubbornly waged. The legend of St. George the Dragon-slayer is a mythic reference to that struggle, with the huge, snake-like monster representing the Old Religion. (Snakes were common symbols in the Old Religion of cyclical regeneration, shedding and regrowing their skins; they were often portrayed wrapped around the arms of the Minoan Goddess statues.) St. George, of course, represents the church. In some versions of the legend, the dragon's head grows back, indicating the tenacity of those who held sacred the Earth, the sun, the moon, and the starry heavens, and who observed Her holy days: the equinoxes, the solstices, and their midpoint days.

The best of Christian theology in Medieval Europe incorporated the cosmological wisdom of the Old Religion. The teachings of St. Francis of Assisi, Hildegard of Bingen, Mechtild of Magdeburg, and Julian of Norwich, for instance, all express awe and reverence for the creation. The astounding burst of cathedral-building in Western Europe during the twelfth and thirteenth centuries was dedicated to the Goddess-figure of Christianity: Mary, Queen of Heaven. Moreover, her worshippers usually sited the cathedrals over land or a spring that had long been held sacred to Mother Earth.

Then came the Black Death and the long recovery from losing one-third of the population of Europe.

Beginning in the sixteenth century, we were seduced by the false promise of certitude, the hubris of claims to absolute knowledge, and the tight rationality of mathematics and mechanistic thinking. We were so entranced by the glamour of modern science that it was able to supplant nearly everything that had gone before. What we have ended up with, however, is knowledge for manipulation rather than knowledge for wisdom, as E. F. Schumacher observed. The classical scientific mind-set never had much aptitude for understanding context, especially that of subtle realities, and certainly it is largely responsible for the centrality of "componentiality" and reductionism in modern habits of thought.

The birth of the modern nation-state, the rapacious Industrial Revolution, and the horror of modern warfare on a global scale have all contributed to "the modern condition." We have lost the security of an intact world and a sense of our place in the cosmos—but we have gained, from the proto-modern Enlightenment, the protective ideals of human dignity and human rights. Yet, we have lost a future unthreatened by nuclear holocaust, and we are losing the life-support systems of the biosphere. Clinging to the illusion of modern rationality, we are careening with entirely illogical motions toward species suicide.

How can we counter the anxieties of modern consciousness and the disturbing conditions that cause them?

The first phase of postmodern relief efforts, which may be a long one, should focus on two areas: restoring meaning and empowering people at the community level. The churches and synagogues in every community *could* play a leading role in both areas, but only if they can meet the challenge of restoring rootedness in the cosmos and meaning in contemporary life.

Postmodern religion, of course, will be unable to win credibility as a source of truth unless it drops the patriarchal "shuck 'n' jive." Simply as ground rules, women will have equal participation in ritual (as ministers, rabbis, and priests); language in worship will be inclusive; and the Divine will be considered other than "male" or "female"—or both, if people prefer. The core of the theology should be creation-centered spirituality, the realization that the natural world is the most profound expression of the Divine and should be honored as such. Interest in this kind of spirituality is growing in Catholic, Protestant, and Jewish circles. It involves accurate translation of the Hebrew scriptures with the holistic, creation-centered meaning of the words and attention to the creation-centered wisdom of the teachings of Christ, as well as the works of the creation-centered saints. Most important, as theologian Thomas Berry has noted, is the understanding that "the Divine doesn't create puppets." That is, the unfolding universe was set in play as a dynamic phenomenon—and we, who came out of the fireball and the elements of the Earth's biosphere, are, according to Berry, the self-reflexive function of the universe. We are a part of the unfolding process, inherently linked with the stars, the winds, the rocks, the soil, the plants, and the animals. They are not valueless "resources" that we are to exploit as detached managers for the sake of a GNP. Fed by the contemporary discoveries of postmodern biology, physics, and astrophysics, Western religion can now finally catch up with the cosmological wisdom of native people's spirituality. Welcome home.

Now that we know who we are, what can be done about our sense of loss and powerlessness in the mammoth structures of the modern technocracy? Postmodern politics is finding expression worldwide in the emerging Green movement, a slogan of which is, "We are neither left nor right; we are in front!" One of the central goals of this movement is the expansion in a more participatory direction of what constitutes "politics" in people's minds. In some countries, such as Belgium and West Germany, the Greens have won seats in their national assembly. In every country where Green politics has taken root, the focus is on strengthening the grassroots movements, on building up community-based economics (usually with employee-owned businesses), and often on bioregionalism, a movement to cultivate the sense of "living in place" with awareness of the ecological, cultural, and economic character of one's region.

Sociologists say that the private sphere has been "deinstitutionalized," that the mediating institutions that stand between the individual and the state have been weakened to a great extent. Green politics counters that erosion with the support of participatory community institutions in government, business, food distribution, education, religion, city and regional planning, recreation, and family life. Town meetings have been the occasion in recent years for a bloc of voters, that is, the residents of the town, to declare themselves in favor of a national freeze on the development of nuclear weapons, of making their town a nuclear-free zone, and of divesting municipal interests from the economy of South Africa. Politicians are paying attention to such citizen policymaking at the community level because they fear losing votes. All similar grassroots efforts are part of the post-modern shift in politics.

In countries where Greens have formed a party and won seats—or even have run unsuccessful but attention-getting campaigns—the guardians of the *status quo* are admitting that "the Greens ask interesting questions" about ecologically blind economic policies, the realities of nuclear power, the dynamics of the arms race, the exploitation of the Third World, and other horrors of the modern age.

The largest Green political organization in this country, the Commit-tees of Correspondence,[4] has composed a list of discussion questions called *Ten Key Values*. It is merely a list of questions. But perhaps the most thoughtful way to begin to Green our politics, our spirituality, and all of modern culture is to raise new questions in a postmodern frame of reference:

1. *Ecological wisdom.* How can we operate human societies with the understanding that we are *part* of nature, not on top of it? How can we live within the ecological and resource limits of the planet, applying our tech-nological knowledge to the challenge of an energy-efficient economy? How can we build a better relationship between cities and countryside? How can we guarantee the rights of nonhuman species? How can we promote sus-tainable agriculture and respect for self-regulating natural systems? How can we further biocentric wisdom in all spheres of life?

2. *Grassroots democracy.* How can we develop systems that allow and encourage us to control the decisions that affect our lives? How can we en-sure that representatives will be fully accountable to the people who elect them? How can we develop planning mechanisms that would allow citizens to develop and implement their own preferences for policies and spending priorities? How can we encourage and assist the "mediating institutions"—family, neighborhood organization, church group, voluntary association, ethnic club—to recover some of the functions now performed by govern-ment? How can we relearn the best insights from American traditions of civic vitality, voluntary action, and community responsibility?

3. *Personal and social responsibility.* How can we respond to human suffering in ways that promote dignity? How can we encourage people to commit themselves to lifestyles that promote their own health? How can we have a community-controlled education system that effectively teaches our children academic skills, ecological wisdom, social responsibility, and personal growth? How can we resolve interpersonal and intergroup conflicts without just turning them over to lawyers and judges? How can we take responsibility for reducing the crime rate in our neighborhoods? How can we encourage such values as simplicity and moderation?

4. *Nonviolence.* How can we, as a society, develop effective alternatives to our current patterns of violence, at all levels, from the family and the street to nations and the world? How can we eliminate nuclear weapons

from the face of the Earth without being naive about the intentions of other governments? How can we most constructively use nonviolent methods to oppose practices and policies with which we disagree and in the process reduce the atmosphere of polarization and selfishness that is itself a source of violence?

5. *Decentralization.* How can we restore power and responsibility to individuals, institutions, communities, and regions? How can we encourage the flourishing of regionally-based culture rather than a dominant monoculture? How can we have a decentralized, democratic society with our political, economic, and social institutions locating power on the smallest scale (closest to home) that is efficient and practical? How can we redesign our institutions so that fewer decisions and less regulation over money are granted as one moves from the community toward the national level? How can we reconcile the need for community and regional self-determination with the need for appropriate centralized regulation in certain matters?

6. *Community-based economics.* How can we redesign our work structures to encourage employee ownership and workplace democracy? How can we develop new economic activities and institutions that will allow us to use our new technologies in ways that are humane, freeing, ecological, and accountable and responsive to communities? How can we establish some form of basic economic security, open to all? How can we move beyond the narrow ''job ethic'' to new definitions of ''work,'' ''jobs,'' and ''income'' that reflect the changing economy? How can we restructure our patterns of income distribution to reflect the wealth created by those outside the formal, monetary economy: those who take responsibility for parenting, housekeeping, home gardens, community volunteer work, etc.? How can we restrict the size and concentrated power of corporations without discouraging superior efficiency or technological innovation?

7. *Postpatriarchal values.* How can we replace the cultural ethics of dominance and control with more cooperative ways of interacting? How can we encourage people to care about persons outside their own group? How can we promote the building of respectful, positive, and responsible relationships across the lines of gender and other divisions? How can we encourage a rich, diverse political culture that respects feelings as well as rationalist approaches? How can we proceed with as much respect for the means as the end (the process as much as the products of our efforts)? How can we learn to respect the contemplative, inner part of life as much as the outer activities?

8. *Respect for diversity.* How can we honor cultural, ethnic, racial, sexual, religious, and spiritual diversity within the context of individual responsibility toward all beings? How can we reclaim our country's finest shared ideals: the dignity of the individual, democratic participation, and liberty and justice for all?

9. *Global responsibility.* How can we be of genuine assistance to grass-roots groups in the Third World? What can we learn from such groups? How can we help other countries make the transition to self-sufficiency in food and other basic necessities? How can we cut our defense budget while maintaining an adequate defense? How can we promote these ten Green values in the reshaping of global order? How can we reshape world order without creating just another enormous nation-state?

10. *Future focus.* How can we induce people and institutions to think in terms of the long-range future and not just in terms of their short-range selfish interest? How can we encourage people to develop their own visions of the future and move more effectively toward them? How can we judge whether new technologies are socially useful—and use those judgments to shape our society? How can we induce our government and other institutions to practice fiscal responsibility? How can we make the quality of life, rather than open-ended economic growth, the focus of future thinking?

NOTES

1. *Individual-liberationist* is a term coined by Harry Boyte and Sara Evans in "Strategies in Search of America: Cultural Radicalism, Populism, and Democratic Culture," *Socialist Review* 75/76 (May-August 1984), 73–100.

2. Peter Berger, Brigitte Berger, and Hansfried Kellner, *The Homeless Mind: Modernization and Consciousness* (New York: Random House, 1973).

3. Marija Gimbutas, *The Goddesses and Gods of Old Europe, 6500–3500 B.C.* (London: Thames and Hudson/Berkeley: University of California Press, 1974).

4. The Green Committees of Correspondence, P.O. Box 30208, Kansas City, MO 64112.

3

A
POSTMODERN VISION OF
SPIRITUALITY AND SOCIETY

Joe Holland

When you send forth your spirit, they are
created, and you renew the face of the
earth.

—Psalm 104, v. 30

INTRODUCTION

Part I of this essay explores the crisis of modern culture with reference to
the conflict between the nuclear and feminine symbols and their setting in
a crisis of modern ideologies. Part II explores the creative face of this crisis
as birthing a postmodern spirituality. Part III sketches a postmodern social
vision. This essay is not so much the argument of a thesis as the sketching
of its vision, assumptions, and implications. [1]

I. The Modern Crisis of Progress

The First World's Cultural Crisis

Contemporary analysis divides the world into three spheres, crudely but usefully described as the First, Second, and Third Worlds. The First World, with the United States at its center, refers to the industrial capitalist nations, which went through their industrial revolutions during the nineteenth century. The Second World, with the Soviet Union at its center, refers to the industrial communist nations, which went through their industrial revolutions during the first half of the twentieth century. The Third World refers to those areas of Africa, Asia, and Latin America that are only now going through their industrial revolutions. In each of these "worlds," there is a distinct leading edge to the social problematic.

In the Third World, the leading problematic is clearly economic. Whatever political or cultural problems are present, the deepest and most immediate issue is the economic suffering of the poor. They suffer and even die precisely because they are poor. Political and cultural oppression, although systemically related, are secondary to this overwhelming economic fact.

In the Second World of the Soviet Union and its satellite nations, the leading edge is political, namely the absence of freedom, including religious freedom. Although this problematic also has serious economic and cultural links, the most obvious struggle is for free space apart from a totalizing state. This is expressed in the struggle for self-determination by religious movements, labor movements, and national movements.

In the First World, however, the leading edge of the social problematic is cultural. Serious economic problems exist, but for the majority economics is not a life-and-death issue. Similarly, serious political problems exist, but we do not yet suffer from a totalized state. Rather, the fundamental issue is the very meaning of modernity, as there is a crisis of progress.

At the heart of culture is spirituality. Every culture is in essence a spiritual (or pseudospiritual) vision of reality. So we might say that if the deepest crisis of industrial capitalism is cultural, we inevitably find a spiritual crisis at its core.

If one were to rank these social problematics according to their order of urgency, primacy would have to be given to the economic struggle of the poor in the Third World and its echoes in the First and Second Worlds, especially among people of color. Second priority would go to the political struggle for freedom in the Second World, and its echoes in the First and Third Worlds. By contrast, the First World's cultural struggle appears an unimportant luxury of the rich capitalist countries.

But to stop with such a competitive framework based on urgency would be a great mistake, for all three problematics are closely related in the integrated experience of modern global society. It is precisely our imprisonment in modern consciousness that makes us see the problematics as fragmented and competitive. It keeps us from the holism of a truly global vision.

The cultural crisis of modern progress is not separate from its economic and political crisis, for it is the meaning of modern economic and political progress which is breaking down. If economic exploitation predominates in the Third World, and political oppression in the Second World, they are both intimately linked to the foundational modern cultural vision, which guided the expansion of industrial capitalism into the Third World, and to the attempt of the Second World to create a still modern alternative in industrial socialism.

So we might say that, from a framework of basic questions, rather than from one of urgent need, the First World's cultural problematic is fundamental, for the First World carries the leading edge of modernity to the entire planet. The cultural crisis of modern progress has profound implications for the economic and political development of the Second and Third Worlds. For the most part, both these areas have uncritically accepted the reigning Western model of technological progress. The hunger of the Third World to break free of First World financial domination in order to unleash its own economic power, and the hunger of the Second World for political and religious freedom from a totalizing secular rationalist state, require not simply economic and political revolution but also a revolution in the cultural foundation of modernity. It is about this cultural transformation that I write here—from within a First World experience, but with wider implications.

The End of the Modern World and the Nuclear Symbol

I propose that in the late twentieth century we describe our historical location as the end of the modern world. This means that we are at the end of that vast cultural project called modern civilization, centered generally in the North Atlantic nations of the West, and in the twentieth century centered specifically in the United States.

This modern project took cultural form from the sixteenth to the eighteenth centuries with the Protestant Reformation and the rationalist Enlightenment. It took political form with the late eighteenth-century American and French liberal revolutions and with their subsequent extension to other countries. It took economic form with the Industrial Revolution of the eighteenth century, the nineteenth-century rise of industrial capitalism, and the twentieth-century rise of industrial socialism.

Ultimately the modern project revealed itself as having one fundamental goal—to emancipate humanity from natural and religious limits. Its ultimate quest, even if not initially clear, was for an autonomously scientific world. Science, and its instrument of technology, become a modern secular religion, aimed at unleashing Promethean energies to solve all human problems and to eliminate all natural limits.

The difference between industrial capitalism and industrial socialism was only one of degree. Initially, capitalism was not fully rationalistic, for it entrusted science and technology to an irrational market, at first still embedded in community and tradition, including the heritage of religious restraints. Industrial capitalism only privatized rather than eliminated religion. Socialism pressed to be fully rationalistic, by bringing the economy under a scientific state, by trying directly to eliminate tradition and to convert traditional community into mass society, and by trying to make religion unnecessary. But later capitalism would catch up with socialism and begin its own rationalistic centralization of power in giant economic and political bureaucracies, supported by militarized states, in turn undermining community, tradition, and religious values by high mobility and consumer propaganda.

Toward the close of the twentieth century we have reached in destructive form the limits of the modern imagination. Seeking originally to liberate humanity, modernity winds up threatening to destroy humanity. We now face the slow threat of ecological poisoning and the rapid threat of nuclear holocaust. In the meantime, great energies of human exploitation, oppression, and alienation are unleashed across the "three worlds."

The modern dream has turned full circle. Seeking to free itself, modern scientific progress has become precariously uprooted—from the earth, from human community and its tradition, and above all from the religious Mystery. Its energies shift from creation to destruction. The myth of progress backfires.

The threat of nuclear destruction (promoted by both superpowers) is a key symbol of the modern cultural crisis. If any doubt exists about this nuclear threat, one has only to read contemporary technical literature. Abundant discussion is found of first-strike capacity, limited nuclear war, and winning a nuclear war. Strategies face questions like the possible need for a preemptive first strike, because waiting for the enemy to attack first might not leave time to retaliate.

Why this sudden intensification of the question? It is not that a more ruthless generation of military strategists has emerged. Neither is it that the military is an evil institution or its members evil people. Such analyses are misguided and even counterproductive. The military forces are no more to blame for war than the police for crime.

Rather the unbridled modern technological drive has pushed the military experience to a new and frightening threshold. The logic of the crisis comes ultimately not from the military, but from the directionless cultural context of late modern technology. In a modern rationalist society, fewer and fewer spiritual guides are found for the technological path.

The Jewish theologian Arthur Waskow has connected the explosion of a nuclear bomb to God's universal covenant with all living things, related in the biblical story of a great flood.[2] In the flood story, God hangs his bow (as in bow and arrow) in the sky as a promise that there will be no chastisement again for the earth. The bow is of course the rainbow which Noah sees. Talmudic elaboration on the story warned that, should severe sin return, the next punishment would not be water but fire. Waskow recounts the fact, told by witnesses of a nuclear explosion, that in the blast all the colors of the rainbow are present, but they are shattered. He proposes then that the bomb itself is the shattering of God's covenant with all living things. It brings the destruction of life—not as the punishment of some distant divine judge, but as the inevitable fruit of humanity's own destructive choice. God's universal covenant with all living things, expressed originally in creation and renewed in the covenant with Noah, is what is really at stake in the nuclear threat.

The Crisis of Spirituality and the Feminine Symbol

The crisis of modern culture is also a crisis of Western spirituality, because modern culture, however much it broke with the religious traditions of the West, has its roots there.

The essence of this spiritual crisis is that humanity's creative energies, granted us by God so that we may become cocreators in the ongoing ecological-historical process of creation, are being perverted into destruction. Modern civilization threatens creation itself. As Pope John Paul II has constantly pointed out in his reflection on modern science and technology, this is the deep crisis of our age.

The turn of modern civilization to mass social and ecological destruction is closely tied to the spiritual flight from the symbol of woman. For this reason, the cultural recovery of the feminine symbol within the heart of the religious Mystery (and the consequent impact on male and female identities) is deeply important in the transformation of modern culture. The classical search for holiness (in all classical cultures, not only in the West) was founded on flight from woman.

In the West, classical spirituality was founded on the Platonic imagery of being liberated from embodiment—rising up to the sky to be free from nature, symbolized by woman. By and large this meant men trying to escape from (and often scapegoating) women, in order to become "holy." For women who would become "holy," it meant escaping from themselves. The classical search for holiness, along with its good and creative side, can thus also be seen as carrying a hidden and negative side, namely a flight from our own bodies, from nature, and from woman.[3]

Nature was symbolized by woman because she could not pretend so easily as man to escape. Woman, as the more visible partner in reproduction, remained the symbol of biological embodiment, of rootedness in nature, and of communitarian tradition. Man could pretend that he played no abiding role in reproduction and after fertilization could leave the rest to woman. The male symbol thus became the image of transcendence of nature—by military conquest, by construction of high civilization, and by the achievement of spiritual "heights." Woman was thus seen as belonging to nature and man to civilization.

By implication transcendence of matter was seen as male, particularly because in classical Western biology the bipolar nature of reproduction was not understood, with the man's seed thought to carry the full life, and the woman's womb only to provide a nest to protect it. Hence, if life was perceived as coming only from the male, the male was consequently perceived as the only authentic image of the divine Source of life.

Yet, even if this was the ideal of classical spirituality, its effect was never fully accomplished. For however much classical spiritual dreamers hoped to escape from the limits of time and space into the transcendence of the universal/eternal, classical civilizations were inevitably bound to the moist and warm "feminine" roots of the earth. Their high culture did not yet have the technological capacity to break with its natural "matrix."

Despite the flight of classical Christian spirituality from biological woman, spiritual man still sought after woman as spiritualized, free of earthiness. The spiritual woman became the Greek *sophia* ("wisdom") or the heavenly Mother of God.[4] Freud, the key figure in the modern interpretration of the psyche, criticized classical Christianity for giving such a strong role to the feminine dimension.[5] Classical Christian spirituality, despite its longing for escape, and despite its overarching patriarchal framework, thus continued in part to honor the feminine.

For example, this residual earthiness is testified to in the religious centrality of the veneration of the Virgin Mary in classical agricultural Catholic societies. Mary provided a vicarious glimpse into the feminine side of the Divine (not fully disclosed in the gender limits of the Incarnation). She expressed in Christianized form the cult of the pre-Christian earth mother. Again, the whole feminine religious symbol was set within a patriarchal context, but it remained nonetheless powerful.

In the modern period, however, this flight from nature took on technological strength, precisely as society was urbanized and as classical spirituality weakened. What the classical world had unsuccessfully tried to do in religious form, the modern world would successfully do in technological form—with catastrophic consequences. Disembodied spiritual energies of transcendent flight from nature were now redirected into scientific-technological conquest of nature. Nature—expressed in the feminine symbol—was now set over against the modern scientific project. But this time it was not a question of rising above nature through religious contemplation, but rather of insulating ourselves from it through external scientific control. Progressively, classical spiritual otherworldliness was converted into modern ecological destruction.

This began with shifts in the imaging of nature by the Enlightenment, as Carolyn Merchant has shown.[6] Nature, which before had been seen partly as a good mother, now came to be seen only as an evil witch to be disciplined and a virgin to be raped. Sir Francis Bacon, the "spiritual father" of the modern scientific method, described his inquiry into nature precisely as sexual plunder.

The public loss of the female symbol had earlier religious roots in Protestantism, where the religious symbol of Mary was officially eliminated, although eventually religion as a whole came to be seen as a feminine womb of refuge from the harshness of public life. In addition, nature was defined as totally corrupt, and the visible structure of the church was not seen as a mediator of divine communion. Finally, Calvinism, by its diminishment of the immanent sense of the sacramental principle, so heightened the transcendent image of God as to divorce God from creation. Later, modernizing strands of Catholicism would follow a similar path of weakening Marian veneration, dissolving institutional mediation, and psychologizing religion into a retreat from the harshness of the political economy.

Both these cultural sources—the Protestant theological interpretation of nature as corrupt and the Enlightenment interpretation of nature as chaos with science as its domination and rape—fed into the creation of industrial capitalism and carried over into its radicalization as industrial socialism. The end result was a hyper-masculinized modern culture whose social projects are increasingly destructive of natural, social, and religious ecology. This brings us, then, to the question of modern scientific ideologies, founded on the modern Enlightenment's view of science.

Faith and Modern Ideologies

The late modern world appears to be limited to a struggle between two materialistic ideologies—industrial capitalism and industrial socialism. The latter constitutes a theoretical materialism, while the former is a practical materialism. But both actually disparage matter, for they both fail to honor its spiritual core. What begins as a rejection of spirit winds up as the degradation and even destruction of matter.

Originally these materialisms were in part a legitimate reaction against the uprooted or disembodied spiritualism of classical Christianity, but now the reaction has become absolute. In their main forms, typified by the two superpowers, both modern materialisms have become blatantly antispiritual, deepening ever more the foundational mechanistic vision of the Enlightenment. They are also profoundly antimaterial, threatening the destruction of the earth.

These two ideologies are in turn played out within church movements as opposing Left and Right positions. On the Right, we have Christian ideological currents adhering to the secularization thesis—the view that the primary crisis is the modern loss of spiritual values. On the Left, we have Christian ideological currents adhering to the relevance thesis—the view that the primary crisis is irrelevance of the classical heritage to modern life. One side seeks to recover classical spiritual transcendence within modern industrial capitalism, while the other seeks a socialist or semisocialist revision of capitalism. Each side in turn is hostile to the other.

Both the modern Left and the allegedly antimodern Right in different ways carry the burden of modernity. They are, in fact, two separate wings of modernity, both climaxing in the maximization of uprooted and destructive technological power. In both cases, authentic culture and its spiritual root are instrumentalized and undermined.

The Left feeds off a despiritualized version of the hyper-masculinized cultural consciousness of modern rationalism. In this sense the Left is the completion of modernity. Although increasingly struggling to wrest itself from this legacy (as seen in its awkward and uneven opening to the feminist, ecological, racial, peace, and religious movements), the dominant form of the Left (whether Leninist communist, social democratic, or social liberal) remains highly scientistic and uprooting in its cultural imagination. It is simply a radicalization of many of the same destructive cultural energies initiated by capitalism—not truly an alternative to them.

The Left leans toward deeper public despiritualization, losing contact with popular religious and social experiences. It often views negatively what appear to be "nonrational" religious energies, expressed, for example, in charismatic or pentecostal form. As a result, the Left often does not know how to drink deeply of spiritual energy. Although it tries to promote justice, it often seems to forget the spiritual source of that defense, or at least not to provide public testimony to the power of the Spirit. Even if the religious Left does not go to the extreme of despiritualization, it seems to deepen the process of religious privatization, especially regarding sexuality.

Of course, the Left is correct in its judgment that classical spirituality alone is not adequate to contemporary experience. Disembodied transcendence cannot be our sole spiritual foundation in a postmodern world. The rationalist critique, therefore, had a point. But society cannot live forever on critique.

The Right apparently attempts to resist modernity in the "private" sexual-psychological sphere, but only to provide discipline and legitimation for the free-market and militarized structures of advanced capitalist modernity. In this sense, the Right is an incomplete form of modernity, but in some ways a more powerful one. At the same time when modernity enters its cultural crisis, the Right attempts to prop up its capitalist wing with a return to classical authoritarian legitimation, this time linked to the national security state. This appearance of a critique of modernity actually protects its destructive engine.

Even the Right's resistance against personal modernization in sexuality and religion is often a destructive attempt to recover a nostalgic past. For example, the Right tries to return to a patriarchal family, precisely when new patterns of shared partnership in marriage may be the only hope for sustaining family in the midst of great crisis. Similarly, the Right heightens the traditional religious image of God as a male warrior-king totally above and so outside creation, precisely when the healing disclosures of God seem now to come to us in the images of nature, woman, peace, and justice, revealed first in and through creation.

Our deepest task, therefore, is not to choose between two fragmented modern ideologies in their common moment of crisis, that is, between a religiously alienated capitalism or a despiritualized socialism, but to transform modernity itself. This means moving toward a holistic postmodern social and spiritual vision of the world, embracing the spiritual reenchantment of life as linked to a vision of social justice.

But linking the two does not just mean hooking the Left's view of a just society with the Right's view of a religious culture. The social vision of the Left is not adequate, nor is the religious vision of the Right. Nonetheless, from the Left we need to take the sense of social justice, and from the Right the sense of public religion, but the content of both needs to be transformed—thus the depth of our modern cultural crisis.

Let us look now briefly at the projected postmodern transformation, first its spiritual side and then its social side.

II. Postmodern Spirituality

In addressing spirituality here, I am not unfolding a Catholic spirituality of the mystery of the Jesus event, but rather attempting to sketch the natural theology that a postmodern theology of any religious tradition would take as its ground. Such a natural theology, functionally akin to the classical doctrine of natural law, could provide the common basis across religious traditions for social dialogue and strategy—what the classical tradition called the pursuit of the common good.

I propose four principles as grounding a postmodern spirituality: (1) the primacy of spiritual energy; (2) spirituality as embodiment; (3) nature as spiritual embodiment; and (4) society as a human expansion of nature's spirituality.

The Primacy of Spiritual Energy

The first principle is the primacy of spiritual energy. The foundation of all social energies—economic, political, and cultural—is spiritual. Spiritual energies and social forms constitute a single whole. Spiritual energies are the deepest source of the legitimation or transformation of society.

The primary task of religious professionals, therefore, is to address this symbolic-spiritual terrain. This does not mean that we should abandon social action, but that we need to become much more conscious and explicit—including publicly—about the spiritual source, ground, and goal of social life. In sum, we need to recover or deepen in our public discourse the symbolic language of spirituality.

Modernists often have trouble with this. The difficulty flows from the fact that modernists have committed themselves to the calculating rationalism of the West's modern scientific project. Modernists plan and strategize almost exclusively out of the left hemisphere of the brain. Such calculation is important, but not everything, nor is it the way the Spirit often works.

The Spirit, to whose power we are opened in prayer and abandonment, often works by surprise rather than planning. If our calculating side is strong, the Spirit may speak to us precisely in the failure of our planning.

I suspect this is why many modernists are so frightened by charismatic or pentecostal energy. It challenges the modern principle of autonomous rational (that is, professional) control. Such spiritual energy cannot be planned, cannot be rationally controlled. Perhaps we sometimes resist the Spirit precisely because we live so much in the ethos of professionalism, because we are so oriented to professionalized rational control—in other words, to *our* control.

I point to three distinct forms of social and religious organization, noting the way they bear on this question of modernity and its expression in professionalism.

Premodern classical society was not oriented to professionalism but to *authoritarianism*. Pyramidal order was its form of organization, cyclical tradition its extension through time, and absolute rule its governance. Religious consecration was its legitimation. This is what modernity reacted against.

Modern society, and to a degree modern religious organization, is oriented to *professionalism*. Bureaucratic rationalization is its form of organization, linear progress its extension through time, and manipulative management its governance. Professional competence is its legitimation. Modernity has been drawn to this.

Postmodern organization, however, will be different still, oriented to the principle of *creativity* (or better *cocreativity*). The holistic web of community is becoming its form of organization, a rhythmic spiral its extension through time, and artistic imagination its norm of governance. As a result its legitimation will come primarily from charism, which is at once social and spiritual. Consecration and competence will not disappear but will be placed at the service of the creativity of charism.

Again, the charismatic principle is the principle of surprise. The Spirit blows where She will, and often beyond our apparent order or well-laid plans. (I say "She" because the creative presence of the Spirit is now linked to the cultural recovery and transformation of the feminine symbol.) This is the essence of creativity, that it cannot be controlled or produced. It emerges. We are not to abandon control and planning, but neither should we limit ourselves to them.

Embodied Spirituality

Postmodern spirituality can be described as embodied. It contrasts with the classical ideal of disembodied transcendence. In no way do I wish to deny the abiding truth of a transcendent vision of God, but our vision of spiritual energies needs today to be rerooted in matter: first in the matter of our bodies, then in our social context, and finally in our natural matrix. Matthew Fox has described this rerooting as a creation-centered spirituality.[7]

Body, society, and nature (in both their structural and historical dimensions, all part of a single whole) are the primary mediators of the Mystery to us.

Turning for a moment to a Catholic perspective which accepts the complementarity of grace and nature, I would like to note that such a creation-centered spirituality is the natural ground within which the subsequent mediation called *grace* appears. Grace is not set against our natural experience, but heals and deepens it. Grace is re-creation of creation. This is also the classical Catholic understanding of grace, deepened however by the sense of history coming to us in religious but negative fashion from the Reformation (as God's judgment on present history) and later in positive but rationalist fashion from the Enlightenment (as modern progress).

We first know God's creative presence in the reality of our own bodies—flesh, blood, breath, nerves, bones, muscles, posture, digestion, sexuality, psyche, etc. This is why our own bodily experience, for example, sexuality, takes on such spiritual and moral proportions, something modernists generally fail to recognize. Our own body is our first religious encounter with the Mystery expressed in creation. Hence, a religious or even an antireligious drive based on rejection, abuse, trivialization, or forgetfulness of our own body would be a denial of our first and abiding encounter with the Creator Spirit.

Our bodies then are not simply "temples of the Spirit" like some external box housing a foreign body. Rather they are dwellings created by the Spirit itself. They express the Spirit's own creativity and reveal her powerful presence, True, our bodies are wounded by sin; yet the Spirit leads us not to escape from the wounded body, but to its healing.

It has been one of the blessings of the modern sexual revolution to recover our sense of sexual embodiment. Similarly, modern feminist spirituality has resisted the degrading of women's bodies and celebrates embodiment. Of course, destructive strains exist in the modern sexual revolution, as well as in modern feminism. But we would miss the healing presence of the Spirit if we failed to open ourselves to the positive side.

Perhaps a special note of embodiment being discovered today is the mutual creativity of the male/female polarity. The gift of bipolar sexuality in nature is precisely to be creative, that is, to give new life. Without this polarity nature yields no new life, and all would be extinguished in permanent death. But the postmodern imagination is expanding the biological creativity of the sexes to social history.

Classical society, apart from the act of biological conception, divorced these male/female principles. As mentioned earlier, it identified the female symbol with nature and the male symbol with disembodied spiritual transcendence (expressed both in ascetic holiness and high civilization).

Modernity tried to end the sexual segregation, but by democratizing woman into the hyper-male ethos of nonregeneration. This began by redefining science as an external act over and against "female" nature, and by converting "male" spiritual transcendence into secular scientific domination. Simultaneously modernity privatized spirituality into the receding feminine symbol, and then began to crush it. It tried to separate the deep meaning of sexuality from the biological renewal of life. Cultural neoconservatives have accurately critiqued the modern privatization of sexuality, but unfortunately their solution attempts to return to the alienation of the classical imbalance of the sexual symbols.

Fresh energy, both spiritual and social, seems to flow precisely where woman and man cooperate in a new way, where (to use the Jungian symbolic rather than strictly biological terms) man recovers his female shadow as roots in nature, and where woman discovers her male shadow as presence in history. Of course this does not mean that men and women simply trade places, with men taking up only reproduction and women only production, but rather a new partnership between the sexes in both nature and history. Neither does it mean that all concrete men and women fit these symbolic types; rather, the meaning is for social structures and their symbolic foundations.

Nature as Spiritual Embodiment

So, too, are we embodied in nature. Our bodies are but the starting point of our corporate and historical embodiment in the whole earth process, and indeed in the process of the entire universe. In the biological and social experience of our bodies, we commune with all nature and history. Classical spiritualities attempted to rise above the limits of nature through contemplation of a disembodied, transcendent universal/eternal. This religious vision, uprooted from time and space, came from the classical Greek ideal. By contrast, modern rationalism tried to insulate itself from nature by fabricating a totally artificial environment. Nature was seen as plastic (as history became social engineering), climaxing in the present destructive threat to our natural, social, and spiritual ecology. As a healing response, the postmodern sense of embodied spiritual energies accepts and enjoys its oneness with the rest of nature and opens itself to the power of rooted history.

The American Indian theologian Vine Deloria wrote that white men of the West are afraid to die because they must finally recognize their oneness with the earth.[8] In our modern Western culture, a deep fear of our earthiness seems to exist, although the fear is weakening. Gratefully, the ecological movement is teaching us once again this ancient lesson, which native spirituality never forgot.

Unfortunately, both Left and Right variants of the cultural ideal of industrial modernization (either in capitalist or socialist form) have carried little ecological sense, and have inevitably seemed fearful of the real history of rooted culture. They have set themselves over against the earth, and so have yet to learn the ancient lesson of Native American peoples.

For this reason, modernists have failed to give meaning to the life and death of ordinary people. Only those who can dramatically change history, and so qualify as "heroes," are granted real meaning. The symbol of the hero, rooted in the classical tradition, is of course the first (perhaps necessary) moment of the male break with nature, community, and authentic mutuality. Modernity, precisely because it rejects nature for history and tries to make all history into heroic history, fails to replace the natural cyclical religious rites of passage among ordinary people. Modernity can appropriate certain rites of community from religion, but not rites that address the very ordinary yet mystery-laden natural experiences of birth, puberty, marriage, illness, and death.[9] Such a modernist vision of heroic history carries the same fear of nature pointed to by Deloria.

The earth itself, an extension of our own biological embodiment, is then our second encounter with God. Ancient peoples saw in the earth a disclosure of the female side of the divine, although their temptation was to worship the earth itself and to sacrifice humanity to it. Christians believe that God is greater than the earth, but our theology has often forgotten how the earth reveals God. The earth is an image of God, of God as mother, a vibrant witness to God's lifegiving presence.

We might call it a foundational natural sacrament. It is a living expression of the Spirit's creativity. That creativity is expanded in humanity and its history, but the history of humanity is in turn an expression or consciousness of earth's own creativity.

This creative revelation of the Spirit is not just a creativity that happened long ago, like the modern deist clockmaker who left the product to run on its own. No, the creative presence of God is brought to us every day in the living earth process, and more broadly in the living universe, where the Spirit gives and renews life. The process of God's creating is ongoing.

We really know this, despite official theologies that forget to remind us. We know that we meet God in the rising or setting sun, in the still or rippling leaves, in the calm and storm of the sea, in the light of day or darkness of night. Indeed, we know that we meet God everywhere in everything.

Society as Human Expansion of Nature's Spirituality

The third embodiment is society, expressed through time as history and crystallized into institutions and their traditions. Institutions and traditions are two dimensions of the same thing, institutions being the structural form of society and traditions their historical narrative. Society cannot exist without these crystallizations. The word we use to describe this human creation of institutions and their traditions is *culture*.

Thomas Berry has sketched postmodern culture as the spirituality of an Ecological Age.[10] He explains how the ecological spirituality of embodiment follows upon three earlier cultural/spiritual phases of human development: first, the primal tribal age with its shamanic forms of religious experience (with nature as the realm of spirits); second, the classical age, which yielded the great world religions (based on transcendence of nature); and, third, the modern industrial age in which science and technology became a rationalist public religion (based on external control and eventually threatening destruction of nature). Only now, at the end of the modern age, do we discover an ecological spirituality of embodiment (creative communion with nature's spirituality).

Human culture in turn is seen by Berry as rising out of three earlier phases of nature's developmental cosmology: (1) the formation of the galactic systems; (2) the formation of the earth within the solar system; and (3) the emergence of life. Finally comes the rise of consciousness expressed in these stages of human culture and its spiritualities.

The cultural consciousness of the Ecological Age centers for Berry on three values inherent in the developmental process of the entire universe, namely differentiation (the multiplicity of life forms), subjectivity (the interiority of all things), and communion (the unity and love of all life through communication).

The modern age has aggressively distinguished itself from premodern tradition and its institutions, as well as from its roots in nature, but it has failed to reconstruct a higher communion with them. Yet they are its roots and the deep source of its abiding energy. Modernity has been hostile to both the traditions and institutions of all past human cultures. This is the root of the antisocial thrust of modernity.

For example, the family has been criticized as patriarchal, religious institutions as alienating, and patriotism as regressive. These rationalist critiques are legitimate to a point, but when absolutized, as they often are by modernists, they grow destructive rather than constructive. They become the expression of manipulative ideologies seeking to uproot society from its institutional ecology of living traditions. Pushed to the level of ideologies, they erode the foundation of society itself. It is the same process of uprooting from natural ecology, now applied to the social ecology of institutions and their traditions.

As the culturally radical wing of modernity, the socialist movement has most obviously failed to appreciate the wisdom embodied in the traditions and institutions of human culture. Admittedly, this wisdom is often hidden by the distortion and overlay of sinful domination (leading especially to the failure to change and to grow), but the healing task is to recover the wisdom so that it may change and grow, not to destroy the root.

Caught in the expansion of its legitimate critique into a total ideology, the socialist movement seldom recognizes within society the abiding, sedimented corporate praxis of ordinary people. The Left thus fails to appreciate the complex and dense layers of social fabric woven into the institutional and traditional interstices between individual and collectivity, and between past and future. The Left wants always to build things entirely new—new unions, a new church, a new "man." It forgets the ecological principle that the new grows only out of the old, even when it appears to break with it. By its desire for total newness, its focus on the individual/mass structural dialectic (individualism for the intelligentsia, mass movements for the others) and an antagonistic interpretation of future versus past, the Left often appears to popular culture as arrogant, elitist, and eccentric.

The same rejection of the mediation of tradition and its populist institutions occurs under capitalism as well, but in a more subtle and therefore perhaps ultimately more corrosive way. For example, Soviet communism has historically mounted a bold ideological frontal assault on religious tradition and religious institutions, but because the attack is so obvious it seems to be losing the cultural war (if Poland has any wider meaning). By contrast, American capitalism does not mount a formally political assault on religious tradition and its institutions, but works more insidiously through cultural propaganda of the consumer society. Religion, family, and tradition all seem to be honored; yet, they are constantly undermined. Although they may flourish as private values, they are increasingly locked out of the public culture. Religion is not directly attacked, but indirectly rendered socially impotent. With the advent of satellite television, the cultural subversion of capitalist modernity becomes ever more powerful on a world scale and reaches deeper into the sphere of familial intimacy.

When religious social action accepts the cultural mis-wisdom of modernity, it too forgets that tradition and its institutions, such as family and church, are the third place we meet God. Focusing only on politics and the state as the carrier of social change, religious social action may forget the spiritual role of these important mediating institutions as historical-structural embodiments of the Spirit's cocreativity with humanity, growing out of the Spirit's cocreativity with nature. By so doing, religious social action would collapse into the cultural crisis of modernity.

This third or historical mediation of our spiritual encounter with God (through society, including its institutions and traditions) begins at the micro-level within the sphere of intimacy—family and friends, neighborhood and small community. Later it expands to the macro level—village, town, city, state, nation, world. These are the places where we meet the living God, or substitute our own distortions of God's presence. In either case, the religious dimension in these objective structures is inescapable. When not distorted by sin, these are the places where the corporate and historical dimension of God's cocreativity with humanity is crystallized and publicly expressed.

But institutions and their traditions can and do become sinful, especially when they fail to grow, thus taking life rather than giving it. Again, the task in this case is not to destroy the institutions and their traditions, but to transform them by healing. Healing in turn does not mean simply a return to old ways, for a healed life gains new energy to grow into a new stage.

These three areas of experience, then—our body, nature, and society—are the natural basis in creation of our encounter with God; all three areas are parts of a single whole. It is here that grace works as well, for grace once again is the re-creation of creation.

How important to remind ourselves over and over again that we do not meet the Spirit simply as created meeting Creator. Rather—and here is the marvel—we are cocreators of our bodies, of nature, and of society. We nourish and expand the physical and spiritual journey of our bodies. As part of the ecology of all life, we join in the mystery of sexuality to nourish and expand the life process against death. And finally, precisely as humans, we consciously nourish and expand our social history into living institutions and living traditions.

But if we are to do all this with authentic creativity, we need always to remember our roots in nature (from which humanity can never be detached), our roots in society both in its historical and structural dimensions (from which our personal identity can never be detached), and the mysterious depth of those roots in the Creator. We thus meet God not simply as creatures but also as cocreators in the creative communion of ecological, human, and Divine life.

Of course, we can resist or even destroy the Spirit-filled communion of creation. This is sin. Yet the creative Spirit is more powerful than our sin, for She comes to heal and transform it. Again, this transformation comes not by fleeing from embodiment, but rather by accepting it more profoundly. Human sin is a rejection of the mystery of embodiment; grace is a more profound return to embodiment.

The destructive energies of our now crisis-ridden modern world are again captured especially in the nuclear antisymbol, for the nuclear threat is the ultimate attack upon all living embodiment on the planet. By contrast, the healing energies of creation and re-creation are revealed in the symbol of woman as life-giver and healer. The mysterious disclosure within the symbol of woman is, in turn, expanded to both sexes, female and male, as true partners in nature and history, both revealing, through the mutual creativity of their images, the mutual creativity of the female and male images of God.

III. THE POSTMODERN SOCIAL VISION

If spiritual embodiment is a key phrase on the spiritual side, creative community, or communal creativity, is the key phrase on the social side. Both are expressions of postmodern holism. Around this social theme of creative community there are specific principles in the three structural areas of economic, political, and cultural life.

The principles applying to these areas will guide the construction of a postmodern society within the womb of the old modern one. The strategy informing them is not the industrial capitalist vision of freeing up the market to maximize autonomous productivity, nor the industrial socialist vision of gaining state power to transform the whole society. Rather, the problematic is more organic and complex, and especially cultural.

Economics: Appropriate Technologies and
Communitarian Cooperatives

The economic thrust embodying community is carried by two distinct but related principles: first, appropriate technologies; second, a renewal and transformation of the cooperative movement.

Both capitalist and socialist societies have constructed an antagonistic relationship to nature, based on the Enlightenment vision of science as the rape-like torture of nature. In the process both forms of industrialization have threatened our natural ecology and alienated human work from its natural, social, and religious roots.

Similarly neither capitalist nor socialist economies seem to be organized around a human community of work. In the capitalist sphere, labor is a commodity to be bought and sold in the scientific market at the lowest price, while in the socialist sphere it is a force to be guided by the scientific state. Both ideologies, in turn, subject labor in the work process to the manipulative control of Taylorism (time/motion studies), now enhanced by cybernation. This subjection has further alienated the labor process.

As a result, we are threatened with degraded forms of work, of which people must nonetheless make the best (a tribute to human creativity). People often seem forced to diminish their own creative energies in the labor process by alienating themselves from natural, social, and religious communion. Pope John Paul II's encyclical *Laborem exercerns*, criticizing the failure of capitalism and socialism to respect the priority of labor, is an important analysis of this alienation. [11]

By contrast, we have new experiments in appropriate technologies seeking to reintegrate the process of human work with its natural communion. One thinks for example of the writings of E. F. Schumacher and his disciple George McRobbie. [12]

Especially important in this regard is the search for alternative energy systems and for new ways of conserving energy. The petroleum-based energy system, now supplemented by the destructive nuclear system, is leading the world into deeper militarization as part of the struggle over strategic resources. The same is true for our whole agricultural and industrial systems, which are increasingly based on petroleum and nuclear energy.

The growing tensions between the superpowers seem less an ideological battle and more simply a battle to control this global supply of limited strategic resources needed for the industrial model. Quite logically, therefore, the two military hotspots of the world—the Middle East and the Caribbean Basin—are both major sources of petroleum. Only when we have more ecological and, consequently, self-reliant energy sources, especially solar, will the foundation be removed for this growing militarization of politics.

Furthermore, the social form of the work process is equally destructive, not only treating people as instruments of capital or the state, but more seriously marginalizing whole sectors of labor from any productive role.

Permanent large-scale structural unemployment is now a horrendous fact across the globe.

For this reason, we must find new ways of organizing human labor into democratic or participatory cooperatives, where human dignity can be better respected, where decisionmaking roles can be more widely shared, and above all where the dormant labor of the unemployed can creatively express itself in meeting basic human needs. Here one thinks of experiments like the Basque cooperatives centered in the town of Mondragon, and the many reflections and experiments on economic democracy. [13]

Politics: Community and Networking

If appropriate technology and communitarian cooperatives are the leading economic principles of a postmodern society, then its leading political principles are the defense or rebuilding of rooted communities and the expansion of international networks of solidarity among rooted communities. Several church phenomena come to mind here as reflecting this postmodern political model.

I use *political* not in the limited sense of the state and modern parties, but in the wider sense of the organizational form of a society. As such, the term applies to organizational forms of the church as well, namely its polity. These church experiments, in turn, are echoes and seeds of wider social creativity.

First, we see the rise of the pastoral strategy of building basic Christian communities, creating, in effect, a new small-scale unit of the church itself. The parish does not disappear, but becomes an outer circle providing certain supplementary or subsidiary functions, yet not intruding on the new decentralized expression of religious energy. For Catholicism, this is a fundamental shift from the Counter Reformation pastoral strategy which, in fear of the Reformation, tried to uproot pastoral practice from the kinship system and to organize it into highly controlled administrative units administered exclusively by celibates. (Celibacy had not been fully enforced for the nonmonastic or ''secular'' clergy prior to this point. The Counter Reformation administrative model was, in turn, a key root of modern bureaucratization.)

Second, we find the rise of the community organizing movement, sponsored predominately by the churches. This new wave of organization parallels the earlier wave of union organization in the workplace. [14]

Third, we see the rise of vast networks of international solidarity, linking groups in struggle across the globe. Much of this is focused on First World solidarity for Third World struggles, but hopefully it will grow to mutual solidarities within and among the First, Second, and Third Worlds. This would mean developing a truly holistic global perspective, linking the economic crisis of the Third World with the political crisis of the Second World and with the cultural crisis of the First World.

But we are still far from that. For example, few U. S. defenders of the poor in Latin America seem concerned to build solidarity with the cause of Polish workers, or vice versa. The Catholic Church overall, as one of the few major transnational actors in the world, has been a key, if inconsistent, promoter of this solidarity.

The interesting thing about this postmodern political energy is that it is positioned on the two flanks of where most modern political energy has been directed. Modern political energy, whether capitalist or socialist, has been largely oriented to the nation-state, expanding in distinct ideological ways the power and competence of the national state. In the process, it has been uprooting the state from community and pitting nation-states against one another. By contrast, the new energy, while not rejecting the national state, directs its energy to these two neglected flanks, local community and global solidarity. It may be, then, that the postmodern period will mark the limiting of the sovereignty and centralization of the nation-state in favor of more organic and creative multiple levels of community from the local to the national to the international.

The other political shift affects the nature of democracy. Throughout the modern period, democracy has been largely representative. This was a necessity of the limits of the technology of transportation and communications. Information, travel, and decisionmaking could not be broadly diffused. Large political bureaucracies, paralleling or absorbing the large economic bureaucracies, were created to mediate the political process.

In the postmodern period, however, participation is becoming more direct, more organic, less hierarchical, less bureaucratic—in sum, more participatory. This expanded participation requires a decentralization of the bureaucracies, a diminishment of the hierarchies, and a turn to multiple levels where priority is given to broadly diffused, small-scale, yet organically coordinated networks of decisionmaking. It is a shift to a cellular mode of web-like process. Again, the foundational explanation for the shift is the more decentralized communications and transportation system (the "information society"), which brings formerly remote areas into the mainstream. This development also begins to undermine the modern rural/urban dichotomy.

Culture: A New Root Metaphor

With this theme of postmodern culture, we return to the original reflection on spirituality. Culture is ultimately a spiritual vision of the structure and process of reality, as well as of its source, ground, and purpose. Modern culture has been ever more aggressively shaping our experience according to a vision that sees reality like a machine. This vision has been described by Gibson Winter in *Liberating Creation* as a mechanistic root metaphor. [15] This mechanistic vision still lies at the foundation of modern understandings of science and, so, of the technological constructs of modern society.

But the modern social machine seems more and more to crush life—natural life, human life, and spiritual life. It threatens to blow us up rapidly or to poison us slowly. In the meantime, it crushes the life of the poor, the unborn, and the dissenters. It seems to render us powerless before colossal economic and political bureaucracies. And worse still, it poisons our value system with the substitute religions of political or commerical propaganda.

The mechanistic vision, which still has a certain value, has now run its course as the ascendant vision of a civilization. Its hegemonic energy is spent. The cultural framework for the future belongs to another vision.

Many people have tried to describe the postmodern cultural vision. From a spiritual viewpoint, I have explored it here as embodiment; from a social viewpoint, as communal creativity. Gibson Winter has described it as drawing on an artistic root metaphor. Simone Weil sought it under the vision of roots. [16] Matthew Fox has described it as a creation-centered vision, Thomas Berry as an ecological vision, and Charlene Spretnak as ecological and feminist. [17]

The above descriptions all reveal important dimensions of the new metaphor. The point is that the metaphor is indeed fresh and is releasing new energy in surprising ways, as well as tapping the deepest spiritual roots of our human tradition. Ultimately it is the presence of the healing and creating Spirit.

NOTES

1. An earlier version of this essay was presented to Catholic religious professionals involved in liberal or Left-leaning social action at a 1983 NETWORK seminar in Washington, D. C., and was published in 1984 by the Center of Concern in its "Occasional Papers" series as "The Spiritual Crisis of Modern Culture."

2. This paragraph comes from personal conversations with Arthur Waskow.

3. I first heard this thesis years ago from Santosh Desai, a Hindu woman who was teaching religion at Saint John's University in New York.

4. For more on this theme, see Susan Cady, Marian Ronan, and Hal Tuassig, *Sophia: The Future of Feminist Spirituality* (San Francisco: Harper & Row, 1986).

5. Sigmund Freud, *Moses and Monotheism*, Katherine Jones, trans. (New York: Vintage Books, 1959). For Freud (the total modern) it was the masculine symbol that was normative, even in religion, which he rejected.

6. Carolyn Merchant, *The Death of Nature: Women, Ecology, and the Scientific Revolution* (San Francisco: Harper & Row, 1980).

7. Matthew Fox, *Original Blessing: A Primer in Creation Spirituality* (Santa Fe, N. M.: Bear & Co., 1983).

8. Vine Deloria, *God is Red* (New York: Dell, 1973).

9. This is especially clear on the Left, which historically has tried not simply to privatize religion but rather to displace it entirely. See David I. Kertzer, *Comrades and Christians: Religion and Political Struggle in Communist Italy* (New York: Cambridge University Press, 1980).

10. Thomas Berry's *Riverdale Papers* (photocopies) are available from The Riverdale Center for Religious Research, 5801 Palisade Avenue, Riverdale, New York 10471. See especially "The Ecological Age," *Riverdale Papers VI*, 1-19.

11. For the text plus a commentary, see Gregory Baum, *The Priority of Labor: A Commentary on Laborem exercens Encyclical Letter of Pope John Paul II* (New York: Paulist Press, 1982).

12. E. F. Schumacher, *Small is Beautiful: A Study of Economics as if People Mattered* (London: Blond & Briggs, 1973), and *Good Work* (New York: Harper & Row, 1979); George McRobbie, *Small is Possible* (New York: Harper & Row, 1981).

13. Derek Shearer and Martin Carnoy analyze many of these experiments in their book *Economic Democracy: The Challenge of the 1980s* (White Plains, N. Y.: M. E. Sharpe, 1980).

14. See Harry C. Boyte, *The Backyard Revolution: Understanding the New Citizen Movement* (Philadelphia: Temple University Press, 1980), and *Community is Possible: Repairing America's Roots* (New York: Harper & Row, 1984), as well as Sara M. Evans & Harry C. Boyte, *Free Spaces: The Sources of Democratic Change in America* (New York: Harper & Row, 1986).

15. Gibson Winter, *Liberating Creation: Foundations of Religious Social Ethics* (New York: Crossroad, 1981).

16. Simone Weil, *The Need for Roots: Prelude to a Declaration of Duties Toward Mankind* (Boston: Beacon, 1955).

17. Charlene Spretnak, *The Spiritual Dimension of Green Politics* (Santa Fe, N. M.: Bear & Co., 1986).

4

TOWARD A POSTPATRIARCHAL POSTMODERNITY

Catherine Keller

They say she is veiled and a mystery. That
is one way of looking.

—Judy Grahn

What is the relation between the quest for a postmodern world and the women's movement toward a postpatriarchal society? We may confidently assert that the desiderata of a postmodern world, as exemplified by the values of the Center for a Postmodern World, bear an intimate resemblance to the worldview emerging as intrinsic to feminist thought and praxis. Both are generating creative alternatives to the traditional (and quintessentially modern) dualisms of body and mind, matter and spirit, self and other, world and deity. Both propose value structures and social institutions based on

63

individuation within a matrix of interdependence, and both hope thus to obliterate relations of dominance and submission. Both generate an organic and interconnected worldsense to replace the depersonalizing individualism perpetrated by a machine economy. But such satisfying generalizations, although perhaps bearing important truths, must work themselves through the specific frictions of our histories, our psychologies, our visions.

The question of the relation between feminism and postmodernity breaks into two antecedent subquestions: Is modernity in any important sense, that is, fundamentally, patriarchal? And is patriarchy fundamentally modern? No suspense need be sustained here. Yes, modernity, as we will see, is intrinsically and not accidentally sexist in its erection of the machine metaphor for the universe, in its assertion of dominion over nature. But no, patriarchy is not essentially modern, for it long predates modernity, which represents only a latest stage of patriarchy. Therefore, from a feminist viewpoint, postmodernity may or may not herald a postpatriarchal age. Because any number of premodernities, reaching back into the prehistorical mists, have assumed and strengthened the dominance of the male in culture and his prerogative to define the roles of both men and women, we can imagine a postmodern patriarchy as well.

But can we really? Or is modernity the end of the patriarchal time line? Androcentric history, beginning in earnest about four thousand years ago, now threatens an imminent apocalyptic climax. Will we need a qualitative leap beyond the world and worldview of sexist ideology in order to avert apocalypse-soon? For technological holocaust is one possible way in which the modern age can end, going out in a grand display of its powers. So if there is to *be* any postmodern world worth calling *world*, is the feminist transformation of culture and psyche perhaps its *sine qua non*—that without which it will not be? *Apocalypse* means, however, not "annihilation" but "unveiling." What does the deep convergence of the woman's movement with the end of the modern age reveal? The answers to such questions are not nearly as evident. To move toward them it will be necessary to explore reasons for the assertions that modernity is essentially patriarchal, but only the latest and hopefully the last patriarchy. Such hope is in a certain sense itself apocalyptic, requiring the end neither of history nor the world but of a particular history and a particular world that have bequeathed themselves to us by way of modernity.

But how do we get there? We cannot simply posit—even with an apocalyptic positivism—our hopes for the world. Utopia is, as *u-topos* tells it, nowhere. To look instead to the beginning, the prefix, consider then the *post* in *postmodern*. It implies a *via negativa*, a negative way of discerning the desired end. It is analogous to the way feminists, including this one, describe our goal as that of a *post*patriarchal world. In both cases there is a surer sense of what we do *not* want to reproduce than of what will replace it. In fact, in both cases a judgment is implied, an account of a deeply problematic, negative character (of either modernity or patriarchy); and so the prefix *post* generates the dialectical tension of a double negative. Somehow out of the energy of critique and consciousness, the vision for the new is to emerge. This is the aspiration—toward something new, the *novum*, the new heaven and earth. Something really *different*, not more of the same. For whatever good might have come of modernity's offering—its emphasis upon democratic equality, its liberation from certain forms of political and ecclesial authoritarianism, the potential and sometimes actual benefits to reason and to real people made by scientific empiricism and technological tools—whatever those contributions are that no postmodernism would want to abandon, a shift of paradigm and of praxis is already happening and must be allowed to happen. With this desire comes a protectiveness, a sense that the new, like a seedling, is delicate and capable of being destroyed (along with everything else). The overweening confidence of a Hegelian dialectic is lacking. This is evident even in the caution the term *postmodern* signals— as though to name too positively the difference coming about might be to foist upon it the same old presuppositions, to crush it inadvertently with our still controlling modernity—not to mention our implicit sexism.

Like the wanderer in Kafka's parable, whose destination is called Away-From-Here, [1] postmodernity points beyond anything we can readily project. It has a quality of Derrida's "destinerrance," a neologism suggesting an errant dispatch with no predetermined destination. Yet Away-From-Here is already somewhere. Pure negation becomes an excuse for agnostic complacency. "Here" is still where we begin, and the history that has brought us here can be criticized, but not dismissed, if we are to find ourselves anywhere else. To cast some light on this mysterious journey, I will examine the relation between feminism and postmodernity in a quite nonlinear way, drawing upon three different areas, or angles, of content and perception. The first will pertain to history, the next to sociopsychology, and the last to worldview and spirituality, all of which will be concluded in an apocalyptic postlude.

I. WITCHMARKS AND THE MODERN WORLD

Modernity comes forth in an emergency of worldview. The Reformation had shattered the organic unity of religion and culture, and Renaissance science was rapidly dismantling the Medieval cosmos. Luther's challenge to ecclesiastical authority and Copernicus's blow of 1543 to the geocentric model of the universe unleash seismic doubts upon an already tremulous sixteenth century. This trauma of the transition of epochs shapes the particular sexism of the modern age.

Although it is true that the church and the culture of the Middle Ages had centered around male figures of authority, we are here pursuing the specific links to our present situation. The dramatic shifts in the Western relation to the natural universe, which characterize the modern epoch, parallel certain significant trends in the understanding of gender. To suggest the way modernity is intrinsically, inextricably patriarchal, I rely upon Carolyn Merchant's *The Death of Nature:*

> The image of nature that became important in the early modern period was that of a disorderly and chaotic realm to be subdued and controlled. . . . The images of both nature and woman were two-sided. . . . Woman was both virgin and witch: The Renaissance courtly lover placed her on a pedestal; the inquisitor burned her at the stake. The witch, symbol of the violence of nature, raised storms, caused illness, destroyed crops, obstructed generation, and killed infants. *Disorderly woman, like chaotic nature, needed to be controlled.*[2]

Yet this defensive obsession with control was not the only option for a modern worldview. Modern science could have followed another route, a path even more faithful to early Renaissance science. Thinkers such as Giordano Bruno (1548–1600) and Leonardo da Vinci (1452–1519) and alchemists such as Paracelsus (1490–1541) had been developing an organicist worldview from elements of ancient gnosticism, the Hermetic mystical traditions, and the emergent natural science. These diverse early Renaissance voices all articulate the view that everything is permeated by life, that nature is itself animate, indeed ensouled. The revival of the Neoplatonic image of the female world-soul accompanied an understanding of nature and the earth as alive and active, rather than passively inert: "Popular Renaissance literature was filled with hundreds of images associating nature, matter and the earth with the female sex. The earth was alive and considered to be a beneficent, receptive, nurturing female. . . . The pervasive animism of nature created a relationship of immediacy with the human being."[3] In the alchemical literature especially, an antihierarchical and antipatriarchal symbolism came to prominence. *Contra* Aristotle, who insisted on the passivity of the female contribution in procreation and the notion of the female as a deformed male (which the Thomist tradition had readily adopted), the alchemists attributed an equal role to male and female principles in sexual generation and, furthermore, developed an elaborate vision of transformation in which images of the androgyne, as the conjunction of equal opposites, played a startling and indispensable role. For Paracelsus, all life proceeds from the eight gnostic matrices, known as "mothers," beginning with the Mother Sophia. However inadequate the symbols of androgyne and Mother Nature may appear when transposed into a contemporary feminist context, they directly counteract androcentric imagery. They represent an importantly subversive trend that might have but did not gain acceptance as the modern worldview. This Renaissance subculture would have developed the organismic tendencies of Medieval thought, freed of much of its authoritarian, dualist, and flagrantly antifeminist superstructures, while pursuing an empiricism in which spirit and nature, and religion and science, would have been richly intertwined. Instead, a science emerged for which nature is seen first as chaotic and eventually, through the work of the eighteenth-century mechanists, as dead.[4] Thus, the metaphor of the machine comes to replace that of the organism. "My aim," wrote Johannes Kepler in 1605, "is to show that the celestial machine is to be likened not to a divine organism but to a clockwork."[5]

Given the protofeminist imagery of alchemy, it is no wonder that the greatest of alchemists, Paracelsus, admitted his indebtedness to the witches.[6] While women labeled "witches" belonged generally to the lowest economic echelon, with no access to education and the written word, many seem to have practiced varieties of holistic and herbal healing. Margaret Murray first proposed the thesis that the witches represent a persistence—in deliberate defiance of the ecclesiastical authorities—of the Old Religion, in which nature was alive with spirits and the deities took both female and male form.[7] Whatever else is true, the witch hunt that ravaged Europe and threatened its female population constitutes the unacknowledged holocaust of the modern age. As many as six million women may have been put to death as witches during the height of the craze, in the sixteenth and early seventeenth century. The *Malleus Maleficarum* was the major textual instrument in the witch hunt, and explained why most witches were female. Kramer and Sprenger's doctrine, that "women are with carnal lust insatiate"[8] and therefore more susceptible to temptation by the devil than are men, ranks as a high point in the history of misogynist theory.

The great European witch hunt is, then, not a phenomenon of the "Dark Ages," but coincides exactly with the dawning of the modern age. Women served *en masse* as scapegoats for the social and religious chaos stirred up by the transition of epochs: they symbolized that which must be either controlled or killed. The mechanical, rather than the organicist, model could rise to prominence because it promised a new, rationally controlled universe, in which no unpredictable spirits or free-willing God could randomly wreak havoc. Yet, the monumental misogyny enacted in the witch persecutions connects even more explicitly to the emergence of modern science.

Merchant shows how misogyny and the subjugation of nature merge thematically in the work of Francis Bacon (1561–1626), that "father of modern science" who so well embodied how "knowledge is power" in his own life, rising to political power from a middle-class origin. Bacon was not oblivious to the witch trials. Indeed, it was his patron, James I, who revoked the relatively mild witch code of Elizabeth I (which had called for the death penalty only in cases of killing by witchcraft). James instituted execution for all practices associated with witchcraft—such as the herbal healing by which many women made their living. According to Merchant, "much of the imagery [Bacon] used in delineating his new scientific objectives and methods derives from the courtroom, and because it treats nature as a female to be tortured through mechanical inventions, strongly suggests the interrogations of the witch trials and the mechanical devices used to torture witches."[9] In the following passage, Bacon appeals to the precedent of torture and trial of witches under the auspices of his mentor, James I, as model for the scientific method:

> For you have but to follow and as it were hound nature in her wanderings, and you will be able when you like to lead and drive her afterward to the same place again. Neither am I of opinion in this history of marvels that superstitious narratives of sorceries, witchcrafts, charms . . . where there is an assurance and clear evidence of the fact, should be altogether excluded . . . howsoever the use and practice of such arts is to be condemned, yet from the speculation and consideration of them . . . a useful light may be gained, not only for a true judgment of the offenses of persons charged with such practices, but likewise for the further disclosing of the secrets of nature. [10]

Bacon does not doubt the reality of witchcraft, despite his modernism, bur rather lauds the witch trials as an opportunity for gaining knowledge, thereby embodying that dispassionate curiosity so cherished in an age of positive science. In saying "drive her afterward to the same place again," he announces the empirical procedure of repeatable experiments by allusion to the capitulation and confession of a witch, in which she "returns" to the crime.

Bacon continues: "Neither ought a man to make scruple of entering and penetrating into these holes and corners, when the inquisition of truth is his whole object—as your majesty has shown in your own example." This sado-sexual imagery indirectly refers to the newly legalized search upon and in the woman's body for "witchmarks," especially in the form of "devil's teats," that is, discolorations of warts found inside an accused woman's labia, which proved her guilty of intercourse with the devil. "The inquisition of truth" cleverly alludes to the various instruments of torture designed especially for women's bodies, in order to extract confession: instruments which would gratify the wildest fantasies of today's patron of pornographic sadism. With such metaphors, Bacon excited support for the new scientific method.

History contradicts the common view that scientific modernity championed the dignity of women and steadily enabled our emancipation from the shackles and superstitions of "the past." And while the defeat of the more animistic science of the alchemical and witch traditions finally undermined the witch hunters, so did it discredit the work of the witches themselves. Their holistic practices were based on a persistence, through the folk traditions, of the organicist image of nature, in which matter is drenched in spirit, and causal interconnections flow among all levels and types of being. The victory of modern science, even if it finally helped to stop the witch hunts of early modernity, only completes the obliteration of this counterculture of women's wisdom. Science comes to a worldview in which nature and women, whose destinies have been linked from the beginning of history, are subject to the manipulation and use of the scientific and technological rationality of the new bourgeois man.

Nor do the late sixteenth and early seventeenth centuries yield any picture of progress in women's social or economic rights. Following the reign of Elizabeth I, for example, the status and rights of wives in England deteriorate, and the family structure becomes steadily more patriarchal and authoritarian than that of the Middle Ages. The kinship bonds of the extended family, so basic to the Medieval economy, begin to give way to the new mobility of the artisan and the merchant. In the increasing isolation of the family, the so-called nuclear family crystallizes, serving to reinforce the authority of the *pater familias*. The shift from a subsistence economy, in which the entire household was economically active, to the economy of an open market based on capital requires segregation of public and private, economic and domestic, spheres. As a result, women plunge into a deeper form of economic dependency than they had ever known.

The emergence of a culture based on capital and competition presupposes a massive philosophical shift in the relation to nature. Mining (previously the cause of much unease for its purported violation of Mother Earth) and production become the key applications of the new machine methodology. Bacon, committed to the acquisition of technologically useful empirical knowledge, would "advise the studious to sell their books and build furnaces" and "forsaking Minerva and the Muses as barren virgins, to rely upon Vulcan." Nature becomes the voluptuous woman to be "forced out of her natural state and squeezed and molded," so that "human knowledge and human power meet as one." [11] But the cosmic machine metaphor will provide the final justification for the exploitation of nature. The theorists of mechanism, Descartes, Leibniz, and especially Newton, forge an ideological framework in which unlimited exploitation of the earth can proceed unimpeded by any holistic sensibilities. Descartes sharply divides reality into rational minds and mechanical bodies. No coherent interrelation can bridge the new dualism. For matter—which had been *mater*, the maternal subject of an uneasy ambivalence—loses its life. Denuded of internal animation, it is cast in the role of a machine, whose separate atoms move inertly in the void. In Newton's words:

> God in the beginning formed matter in solid, massy, hard, impenetrable moveable particles; . . . these primitive particles being solids are incomparably harder than any porous bodies compounded of them. . . . And therefore, that nature may be lasting, the changes of corporeal things are to be placed only in the various separations and new associations and motion of these permanent particles. [12]

Chaos has been successfully defeated; nature and woman are in place for exploitation. The wicked witch is dead. "Nature, women, blacks and wage laborers were set upon a path toward a new status as 'natural' and human resources for the modern world system." [13] In the modern master-fantasy of natural law, the impenetrability of a dead machine had replaced the porousness of the organism.

II. REPRODUCING THE IMPENETRABLE EGO

As the essays in this and the previous volume stress, however, the mechanistic paradigm has been breaking down through recent decades. Concurrently, traditional sexual stereotypes have been failing. Yet, if this culture is getting Away-From-Here intellectually, we remain mired in the Here when it comes to habits of feeling and practice. By what mechanisms does the modern worldview continue to perpetuate itself in our actual lives? Let me trace one of the many social structures that seem, unconsciously and unfailingly, to have been reproducing the mind-set of modern science, economics, and gender relations. This is an institution that crumbles today but has served as our foundation. The self-enclosed family unit, as sociologist Nancy Chodorow demonstrates, is a quintessentially modern phenomenon, subserving a socioeconomic system based on sexism and competition:

> Women's mothering in the isolated nuclear family of contemporary capitalist society creates specific personality characteristics in men that reproduce both an ideology and psychodynamic of male superiority and submission to the requirements of production. It prepares men for participation in a male-dominant family and society, for their lesser emotional participation in family life and for their participation in the capitalist world of work. [14]

What is it about "mothering" that perpetuates the situation of a patriarchal high capitalism (and perhaps any highly bureaucratic and hierarchical society based on technological production)? In a situation in which the father is mostly absent and the mother is all too present, the father becomes inaccessible, abstract, and subject to idealization. The mother, by contrast, will be the emotionally primary parent, appearing dangerously powerful. When male children learn that they must cease to identify with their first parent, the mother, in order to become "men," they pass through a trauma Freud called the "Oedipal crisis." They must identify with a distant father, absorbing his and the society's contempt for the over-present mother. "Thus, boys define and attempt to construct their sense of masculinity largely in negative terms;" [15] that is, they reactively know they are *not women*, but lack a primary bond to the male they are supposed to emulate. Competition with the father plays an important role in the development of masculine personality, yet the alienation it engenders operates more consciously than the repressed contempt for the mother.

The male sense of female inferiority is derived from a deep anxiety regarding the power of the mother. As Karen Horney argues, this more primordial, uncanny "dread of women" arises from the early experience of maternal omnipotence in the situation of primarily female childcare arrangements. The boy's relation to the mother is charged with ambivalence, for he still carries the memory of the primary bond, and with it a tendency to glorify her. As Horney paraphrases it, "There is no need for me to dread a being so wonderful, so beautiful, nay, so saintly." [16] Yet at the same time, women must be labeled as objectively dangerous, destructive, or seductive, for the psychosocial situation requires that the boy remain oblivious to his fear of her: woman counts, then, as objectively threatening. "It is not . . . that I dread her; it is that she herself is malignant, capable of any crime, a beast of prey, a vampire, a witch, insatiable in her desires. . . . " [17]

The motivation behind the witch hunts, during an era in which the traditionally masculine values of dominance over nature, body, and other came to such historical prominence, seems transparent: women's power needed to be at once denied and objectified. The scapegoating of a specific, marginal class of women must have served to alleviate the massive anxiety of transition into modernity.

Men socialized in a situation of early female dominance and male aloofness will be well prepared to assume their positions in a work-world based on the model of dominance and the denial of affective ties. Women, on the other hand, will emerge from the isolated family situation prepared to perpetuate the whole cycle; that is, themselves lacking adequate self-esteem, public importance, and emotional intimacy with men raised to repress feeling, women plunge themselves into the role of mother as a source of prestige and affective intensity. "Women come to mother," according to Chodorow, "because they have been mothered by women. By contrast, that men are mothered by women reduces their parenting capacities." [18] The gender difference cannot be explained in terms of "nature." Rather, girls identify with their mother as not only primary but same-sex parent. Therefore, the daughter will internalize the mother's role as motherer. But in our culture, she will also internalize the mother's low self-esteem and suffer long-lasting difficulty differentiating herself from her mother. Chodorow claims that women thereby develop hostility rather than contempt toward their mothers. As Dorothy Dinnerstein has so well shown, such hostility of the daughter toward the all-powerful mother from whom she cannot free herself translates into a hostility toward women in general, which, ironically, implies self-loathing. Women's socialization undergirds the sexual economics upon which both the organization of gender and the organization of production are based. For "an ideology of women as mothers extends to women's responsibilities as maternal wives for emotional reconstitution and support of their working husbands." [19]

The apparently private workings of the domestic world thus protect and reproduce the interests of the socioeconomic system derived from the metaphor of the machine. The traditional family reproductive unit has reproduced the society of which it is a microcosm. However unconsciously, the psychosocial mechanism of male absence and female presence guarantees a transgenerational production line for patriarchy. Certainly, the machine metaphor of the natural cosmos, along with the presuppositions of sexual hierarchy, have been and continue to be shaken at their foundations in this century. But we may not blind ourselves to the irony of the simultaneous social history: the ever-increasing mobility required by contemporary capitalism is only continuing the breakdown of extended ties with community and family, and so ever heightening the isolation of the family unit. If we hear that the majority of families no longer fit the traditional image of male breadwinner and female caretaker, this can occasion only the most circumspect hope. For most of the situations in which women work also presuppose that women nurture, often without any male coparent at all. Still the mother is primary and the father absent.

The history of the modern family yields consequences not only for the sociology of gender relations but for the very sense of self. According to Chodorow, the asymmetries in the early relational lives of females and males produce profound differences in personality structure: "Boys come to define themselves as more separate and distinct, with a greater sense of rigid ego boundaries and differentiation. *The basic feminine sense of self is connected to the world, the basic masculine sense is separate.*"[20] It would seem that the sense of self inflicted upon males bears a startling resemblance to the Newtonian atom! It is separate, impenetrable, and only extrinsically and accidentally related to the others it bumps into in its void. The advantage of its hardness lies in its apparent power of self-differentiation, in the clarity of boundaries demarcating it from the others. The more fully does a male incarnate this sense of separateness, the more efficiently has he conformed to the machine-economy of modern patriarchy. The components of a machine, unlike the members of an organism, are intrinsically independent of each other, connected only externally. They do not actively and effectively take part in each other's essence. Not interconnecting with each other, they remain rigidly linked according to function.

What of the female self produced by the same conditions? It is no more free from conformity, surely, and no more desirable as an ideal for a postpatriarchal and postmodern personality. Women's focus on connection, on relation, has emerged in a situation that confined her to a narrow set of relations, defined in terms of her capacity to mother. The female self must exert tremendous effort to free herself from relations of dependency and the bondage of symbiosis. Otherwise she lingers in a prolonged identification with the mother, and later feels herself little more than someone's girlfriend, someone's wife, someone's mother. As feminist theology has argued for at least twenty-five years,[21] women's liability, or "sin," lies not in pride, arrogance, separation and other hypertrophic self-assertions, so much as in forms of self-loss, self-abnegation, and passivity.

Women have known relation at the cost of self. But I disagree with Chodorow's assessment that women have had "too much connection and not enough separateness."[22] I maintain instead that women have had too much *dependency* and not enough *self*. Women have had, in fact, not too much but too *little* connection: our spectrum of relationships has been grotesquely confined to the overintensified private sphere defined by the nuclear family. Women have, until recently, lacked any open, public, and adventurous range of relations, in which adequate ego-strength might emerge. No matter how unsatisfactory and unjust most men's work circumstances have remained, men have at least tasted the needed contrast between public and private, breathed the open air on the way to the workplace and enjoyed some form of communication and solidarity with other adults. The lack of a world in which to try our talents has crippled the female self: woman has been a connective being with too few connections. And if selfhood is intrinsically relational, a paucity of relational possibilities will inhibit strength of self. Female connection without deep selfhood, male selfhood without deep connectivity—from neither can come, without a shaking of the foundations, a richly relational self.

Nonetheless there is a clue here, in woman's connectivity, concealed amidst the circumstances that suppress women's self-empowerment.

> From the retention of preoedipal attachments to their mother, growing girls come to define and experience themselves as continuous with others; their experience of self contains *more flexible or permeable ego boundaries.* . . . Masculine personality, then, comes to be defined more in terms of denial of relation and connection (and denial of femininity), whereas feminine personality comes to include a *fundamental definition of self in relationship.*[23]

If there is to be an alternative to the dualism separating us from each other, from our bodies, from our planet, must it not take form precisely—but for both sexes—as a *self in relationship*—a world-connected personality? Is it not precisely the sense of permeability that must be retrieved from the Newtonian atom? Is it not a fundamental redefinition of individuals—selves and atoms—that postmodernity calls forth, a new sense of individuality as arising always within the infinite net of relations? The interrelation of self to self parallels women's sense of intimate connection (but not mere identification) with the body and with the earth. Already endowed with a sense of ourselves as relational beings with fluid boundaries rather than impenetrable walls, women may bear—however devalued, underdeveloped, and self-negating our selfhood has been—the key to a postmodern selfhood. With the ineluctable breakdown of the traditional family, males (beyond those who are exceptionally poetically open) may grasp this possibility for themselves—in male modes.

From the foregoing analysis we can derive this proposition: *Getting beyond the dualisms, the mechanisms, and the hierarchies of modernity will require a radical cooperation of and with feminism.* In a period of conservative backlash, we may need to redouble work to change the sexual economy, taking personal and social responsibility for the results of the gender roles and family structures that reproduce separate, dysrelational male selves, along with subservient female semiselves. Otherwise, alternative ideas will fall like seeds among the rocks and the weeds. As I have argued elsewhere at length, if men must move beyond the "separative" self, women must move beyond the "soluble" self—only then can both genders begin to realize the "connective" self.[24] *Without a deep-rooted collaboration with the feminist project, the current movement toward a postmodern paradigm will be defeated as surely as was the alternative to modernity posed in the early Renaissance by the animistic, Hermetic, witch-related tradition.* For the dualistic and separative selves produced by patriarchal conditions of family and culture cannot finally embody and propagate a nondualistic and connective way of being. *The alternative worldview cannot become a world unless it realizes itself in psychopolitical practice.* Feminism is a *conditio sine qua non*, a necessary if not sufficient condition, of any postmodern world.

III. Cosmos, Goddess, Spirituality

Feminism depends upon the late harvest of many values cultivated in modernity. The Enlightenment commitment to emancipation, for instance, however slow to apply itself to women, determines much liberal feminist rhetoric about equality. Radical feminism often relies on the discourse of class oppression and revolution which springs from the Marxian emanation of Enlightenment thought. The transformation of sex roles seems inextricable from access (in the "first world" middle and upper-middle classes, at least) to a modern technology which can do much of that unpaid labor traditionally assigned to women. Therefore, when I associate feminism with postmodernity, indeed with postpatriarchy, I do not assert that one age emerges in pristine disconnection from the previous age. A new age must use the resources, cull the advantages, and transform the contexts of all that it receives. (Only a patriarchal world is created *ex nihilo*—out of a nothing, a void.) For it is in the cracks of the old world order that the seeds of a new age can sprout.

Perceiving the relevance of the psychological to the cosmological opens the question of the nature of reality—a question that, since the modern age began, cannot be addressed without dialogue with science. How does the feminist commitment to the relational nature of the personality coordinate with nature itself? In the following passage, Whitehead, writing as the outline of a post-Newtonian physics had begun to crystallize (1933), contrasts the new physics to both Newtonian mechanics and "the old common sense doctrine":

> The notion of self-sufficient isolation is not exemplified in modern [i.e., contemporary] physics. There are no essentially self-contained activities within limited regions. . . . Nature is a theatre for interrelations of activities. All things change, the activities and their interrelations. . . . It has swept away space and matter, and has substituted the study of the internal relations within a complex state of activity.[25]

Relation, in other words, is more than a feminine or feminist preoccupation; it is the best metaphor for the nature of the universe. Relativity and quantum theory and, more lately, holography have helped to overthrow the notion of the static atom moving along a predictable pathway in space: there *is* nothing but the process of interrelation. Things *are* processes of connection. Transformation is fundamental to such interrelation; that is, things are not fundamentally separate entities which enter into relationships and undergo superficial changes while remaining essentially the same, self-identical things. Rather, because all entities enjoy "internal relations" with all others in their world, the others are taken into their very constitution. Things enter into each other, they interpenetrate, as influences admitting of no fixed boundaries. I am different now from the one who began this sentence, for boundless influences from the universe, including my past, have entered into me; who I am is how I respond—more or less openly and creatively—to these influences. If, as Whitehead says elsewhere, "the pure conservative is fighting against the essence of the universe,"[26] it is because the conservation of what has been only occurs in the context of the creation of what will be. Nothing remains the same. Are not the rigid ego boundaries held up as the masculine ideal, in opposition to the fluid female processes of relation, not an instance of the "pure conservative"? If so, no wonder males, unconsciously forced to fight "against the essence of the universe," keel over from early heart attacks.

These insights, drawn from the tradition of process thought and its ongoing interpretation of Whitehead and twentieth-century physics, are not foreign to feminist theory. Perhaps Robin Morgan's *The Anatomy of Freedom* represents the most extensive and creative adventure into the interface of feminism and the new science. An activist and poet whose presence has been shaping the current wave of feminist activity from its incipience in the early 1970s, she makes a mockery of the cliché that feminism is a single-issue movement. It is not just a matter of adjusting the relations between men and women in our society: rather, sexual politics mirror the entire complex of human interactions with the universe. "Gender, race, global politics, family structure, economics, the environment, childhood, aging—all reveal their interconnectedness as we move around the holograph."[27] Her book delights in the metaphors of a pan-relational universe emanating from many areas of contemporary science: "The internal workings of the human body or of an atomic particle, of spiritual faith and scientific fact, of aesthetics and astrophysics, disclose themselves as interwoven expressions of one dynamic whole." Moreover, Morgan does not understate the dependence of any viable postmodernity, that is, of any qualitative leap into the future, upon the deep undercurrents of the woman's movement.

> Feminism is, at this moment and on this planet, the DNA/RNA call for survival and for the next step in evolution—and even beyond that feminism is, in its metaphysical and metafeminist dynamic, the helix of hope that we humans have for communication with whatever lies before us in the vast, witty mystery of the universe.[28]

If feminism is indeed the *sine qua non* of a new age, the necessary condition and most vital cause of a postmodern world, the consequences for ignoring the connection would be as monstrous as the hope of realizing it is unlimited. Charlene Spretnak, in *The Politics of Women's Spirituality*, sounds the same dramatic, even optimistic, chord:

> The global feminist movement is bringing about the end of patriarchy, the eclipse of the politics of separation, and the beginning of a new era modeled on the dynamic, holistic paradigm. In working toward these goals, we have many allies among men. Radical feminists envision that era, and the long process leading toward it, as a *comprehensive* transformation.[29]

Only a few years after the publication of this monumental collection of essays on "the rise of spiritual power within the feminist movement," such buoyant confidence has been for many eroded by the state of cultural and political entropy pursued by "the pure conservative." But it is no naive spirit, asserted as it was already after the early 1980s and the defeat of the Equal Rights Amendment; the hope it bespeaks fades only before impatience, cowardice, and cynicism. In an open universe, no outcome is guaranteed: this comprehensive transformation will not necessarily succeed; but it *is* underway. One may presume the outcome will have something to do with whether the interchange between feminism and other proponents of a postmodern world becomes truly reciprocal. Women are heeding the imagery of interconnection; but are other advocates of interconnection, for their part, as fiercely committed to the connection with feminism?

Accompanying the intuition of an interwoven universe, *spirituality* has come to be recognized in the women's movement as a force for world transformation. Many women cannot now find this force within the structures and metaphysics of Christian traditions, as it has largely functioned to sanctify the social *status quo* and to glorify the father as God.[30] Thus the premodern, indeed archaic, image of a Goddess has arisen spontaneously as a spiritual alternative to the old Father-Son dyad. Yet those women within the Jewish and Christian traditions who insist upon gender-inclusive or nongendered pronouns of God involve themselves in the same spiritual project—whether or not they can embrace the fully woman-identified metaphor of "Goddess." It will not help to pose another dualistic exclusivism, of a Goddess versus a male God; but without explicit imagining of the deity in female form, our theological habits will preserve the sanctity of the father over the mother. Nor does such imagining seek to erect a feminized equivalent of the traditional God: a Jehovah with breasts and no beard, to be externalized and worshipped in his *or* her sheer (mere) transcendence—separate, unmoved, and all-controlling. Rather, feminists understand the femaleness of deity or the Goddess herself as *metaphor*.[31]

A metaphor of what? By definition, a metaphor cannot be exhaustively paraphrased; however, I would sort four conceptual strands out of the vast tapestry of meanings the image inspires: (1) *Goddess*—the female face of God—is a metaphor of a woman-identified self, precisely as a self powerful in, rather than disenfranchized by, relatedness—the connected, non-atomic, yet self-assertive and individuating subjectivity we gleaned from our previous discussion of Chodorow. (2) She symbolizes all the power, value, and wisdom culturally repressed in and through the oppression of women. Sometimes this complex of power, value, and wisdom has been called *the Feminine* to distinguish it from particular women. But metaphors do not float free of specific embodiments without becoming stereotypes—thus *Goddess* is an apotheosis of all that has been devalued *in and through* the devaluation of women: difference, emotion, body, nature, cosmos. I suggest that the energy and awareness of that *universal interconnectedness* which the new physics glimpses well approximates her content. (3) She reaffirms that life is irreducible to any set of natural laws or random chances. That is, I argue that atheism—however tempting to many in the light of the Judeo-Christian deification of masculinity—is a banal option for feminism or for the postmodern world. If self and world in women's experience generate new metaphors of deity, why insist these are "just" metaphor? Does not such reduction deflate the metaphors themselves? Goddess-imagery opens new experiences of the divine. (4) The Goddess points forward, into a possible postmodern age, precisely by looping back through a premodern heritage. The premodernity of interest here is prepatriarchy: a probably widespread sociospiritual structure of the Goddess-worshipping Neolithic cultures.[32] (This view leaves about four thousand years of patriarchal premodernity in between.) But this archaic past is less important as factual history or nostalgic myth than as re-membered in the creative reconnecting, which is the essence of *re-ligio*: a "tying back together." This source of female energy, as re-source, does not exist in any literal past, but in the metaphoric ingathering of the present. Female metaphors of deity need not operate out of the energies of exclusivism, of the supremacy of any "we" versus "they." Whether—as Jews or Christians—we place them alongside of depatriarchalized male metaphors of deity, whether for a time we claim primary attention for Goddess-images, whether we prefer genderless abstractions like "light" or "love" to all anthropomorphic imagery, or whether the very discourse of deity is for us dead, we cannot dispense with the religious action of global interconnection. In a consciousness raised by feminism, structured by a pluralistic holism, and enlivened by affective relation to the extended family of the universe, the fullness of the present can yield its own future. Spirit then no longer works against body, for the universe unfolds here and now, from our own flesh. Nor does any central oneness stifle the difference of the many. In the "theatre for interrelations," spirituality—for men as well as women—can only mean centering by connecting, and connecting by centering.

IV. APOCALYPTIC POSTLUDE

The *prepatriarchal* and the *premodern*, like the *postpatriarchal* and *postmodern*, need not date and determine themselves only as negation of the patriarchal and the modern. Rather, the *pre* joins the *post* through a sort of dialectical spring into the future. If, that is, we are to survive into a future at all. To "survive" does not mean merely to endure, but to *"live-beyond"* and so to live better, more abundantly. The survival can no longer be just of the "fittest," that is, by the macho of the most competitively brutal. If the technological aggressions of modernity are to be survived at all, we will be realizing the postmodern vision of an interdependence in which each being has enough resources, and abundance lies in the intensities of interchange. The female, in psyche, society, and cosmic symbol, represents a doorway. It is already in place, held open by the global urgency of women's situations, and by the relational continuum from woman to woman, from woman to man. The endless political, social and spiritual energy of that continuum must not be dispersed by the new witch hunts (as, for instance, against abortion clinics or homosexuals).

   If modernity has landed us at such points of closure as the psychology of the nuclear family and the mechanics of nuclear war, we know ourselves at least at the threshold: of unfathomable destruction or of the mystery of a widespread disclosure. *Apocalypse*, after all, does not mean conclusion or cataclysm, but "revelation"—literally the "removal of the veil."

> They say she is veiled
> and a mystery. That is
> one way of looking.
> Another
> is that she is where
> she always has been, exactly in place,
> and it is we,

we who are mystified,
we who are veiled
and without faces.[33]

NOTES

1. Asked where he is riding to, the speaker responds, "'I don't know, . . . only away from here, away from here, only by doing so can I reach my destination.' 'And so you know your destination?' . . . 'Yes,' I answered, 'didn't I say so? Away-From-Here, that is my destination.'" Franz Kafka, "My Destination," *Parables and Paradoxes* (Berlin: Schocken, 1975), 189.

2. Carolyn Merchant, *The Death of Nature: Women, Ecology, and the Scientific Revolution* (San Francisco: Harper & Row, 1980), 127; emphasis added.

3. *Ibid.*, 28.

4. See David Ray Griffin's unpublished paper, "Theology and the Rise of Modern Science."

5. Quoted in Merchant, *The Death of Nature,* 128–29.

6. In 1527, Paracelsus reportedly "threw all his medical works, including those of Hippocrates and Galen, into the fire, saying that he knew nothing except what he had learned from the witches." Matilda Joslyn Gage, *Women, Church and State* (1893; Watertown, Mass.: Persephone Press, 1980), 104. See Mary Daly, *Pure Lust: Elemental Feminist Philosophy* (Boston: Beacon Press, 1984), 7, 89, 138, 422.

7. Margaret Murray, *God of the Witches*, 2d ed. (London: Oxford University Press, 1952); *The Witch Cult in Western Europe* (London: Oxford University Press, 1921). Present-day feminist followers of Wicca (the way of wise women), or witches, would support Murray's hypothesis, while other feminists, such as Rosemary Ruether, consider it extravagant, and claim that if the witches were practicing a vestigial form of folk religion, it was partly because they had internalized the projection upon them by their persecutors of demon-worship. See Rosemary Ruether, *New Woman, New Earth: Sexist Ideologies and Human Liberation* (New York: Seabury, 1975), 96–97.

8. Kramer and Sprenger, *Malleus Maleficarum*, Montague Summers, trans. (London: J. Rodker, 1928).

9. Merchant, *The Death of Nature*, 168.

10. Francis Bacon, "De Dignitate et Augmentis Scientiarum" (1623), *Works*, Vol. 4 (London: Longmans Green, 1870), 296; quoted by Merchant, 168.

11. Bacon, "Novum Organum," *ibid.*, 247; quoted by Merchant, 171.

12. Isaac Newton, *Opticks*, 4th ed. (1730), query 23(31) (New York: Dover, 1952), 400; quoted by Merchant, 278.

13. Merchant, *The Death of Nature*, 288.

14. Nancy Chodorow, *The Reproduction of Mothering: Psychoanalysis and the Sociology of Gender* (Berkeley: University of California Press, 1978), 180.

15. *Idem.*

16. Karen Horney, "The Dread of Women," *International Journal of Psychoanalysis* 13 (1932), 136.

17. *Ibid.*, 135.

18. Chodorow, *The Reproduction of Mothering*, 211.

19. *Ibid.*, 219.

20. *Ibid.*, 169; emphasis added.

21. Since the classic essay by Valerie Saiving, "The Human Situation: A Feminine View" (1960), reprinted in *Womanspirit Rising: A Feminist Reader in Religion* (San Francisco: Harper & Row, 1979), 25–27.

22. Chodorow, *The Reproduction of Mothering*, 211.

23. Chodorow, 169; emphasis added.

24. Catherine Keller, *From a Broken Web: Separation, Sexism and Self* (Boston: Beacon Press, 1986).

25. Alfred North Whitehead, *Nature and Life* (1934) (New York: Greenwood Press, 1968), 15.

26. Whitehead, *Adventures of Ideas* (New York: Free Press, 1967), 274.

27. Robin Morgan, *The Anatomy of Freedom: Feminism, Physics and Global Politics* (Garden City, N. Y.: Anchor Press/Doubleday, 1982), xv.

28. *Ibid.*, 283.

29. Charlene Spretnak, *The Politics of Women's Spirituality: Essays on the Rise of Spiritual Power Within the Feminist Movement* (Garden City, N. Y.: Anchor Press/Doubleday, 1982), xviii.

30. For the classic exposé of God's fatherhood as the definition of patriarchy, see Mary Daly, *Beyond God the Father* (Boston: Beacon Press, 1973), 19: "If God is male then the male is God."

31. See Nelle Morton, *The Journey Is Home* (Boston: Beacon Press, 1985), 147–49.

32. See also Marija Gimbutas, *The Goddesses and Gods of Old Europe: Myths and Cult Images* (Berkeley and Los Angeles: University of California Press, 1982).

33. Judy Grahn, "They say she is veiled," *The Queen of Wands* (Trumansburg, N. Y.: The Crossing Press, 1982), 12.

5

IN PURSUIT OF
THE POSTMODERN

Richard A. Falk

Once the inevitabilities are challenged, we
begin gathering our resources for a
journey of hope.
—Raymond Williams, *The Year 2000.* [1]

I. MODERN AND POSTMODERN IMAGERY

The challenge of this book and entire series begins with its terminology.
The most extensive discussion of postmodernism has thus far been in literary
and cultural circles. In these settings, the *modern* is associated with an effort to establish an elite set of standards by which to assess the progress of
civilization and to pass judgment upon its deficiencies, especially its emphasis on materialist and technological achievement. The postmodern sensibility registered a strong reaction by way of both taste and values. Postmodernism, in these circles, denies the capacity of language, mind, or spirit
to establish anything by way of standards in an objective manner. It is radically deconstructionist, destroying, if it can, all illusions that anything what-

soever can be singled out as truly significant. This postmodern mode is characterized above all else by a critical turn of mind, both skeptical and ironic. At its best, this postmodern sensibility helps emancipate us from colonizing forms of knowledge associated with both evident and disguised structures of domination: statism, nuclearism, patriarchy, and others.

Now this sense of *postmodern* is quite different from the spirit manifested in this series. This spirit is reconstructionist, optimistic, normative. It does not repudiate the achieving side of modernism, but seeks to displace its negative features. A postmodern possibility implies the human capacity to transcend the violence, poverty, ecological decay, oppression, and injustice of the modern world. The failures of the modern world are here overwhelmingly associated with false and constraining boundaries, the most prominent of which is, of course, the borders of the sovereign state. These false boundaries, then, become springboards for conflict, inducing violence and massive suffering, especially because of the refusal of the larger, more ambitious states to respect the autonomy of other states. Additional false boundaries interact and intensify the forms of conflict associated with the state itself: those of race, class, religion, ideology, gender, language, age, and civilization.

Closely connected with these divisions of the whole that have become invested with emotive content is a series of splittings that underlies the efficiency of modernism, above all, the expropriating potency of specialization of labor and inquiry. This specialization as organizing principle endows instrumental reason with a superior status in human affairs, creating the familiar hierarchical dualism of mind and body, of spirit and flesh, of reason and emotion, of objective and subjective, of thought and feeling. The modernist bias is to act in the world as if these hierarchies expressed and exhausted the real structures of experience, providing both orientation and guidance. Postmodernism, by way of contrast, is trying to "reinvent" reality in more holistic, less hierarchical imagery.

The practical problems of modernity, but not necessarily the metaphysical ones, would be less severe if separateness could be consistently sustained by careful organizing categories, but it cannot. It is the intensifying interdependence of the modern circumstance conjoined to this fierce sense of specific identity that makes the world so dangerous and frightening. Of course, these conditions are aggravated in the extreme by technology and by the cultural reign of mechanistic and reductionistic understandings of science. Most obviously, nuclear weapons as instruments for struggle by part against part dooms the whole, and overwhelms any possibility of modernist sanity: the relation of means to ends is so radically disrupted by insisting that my identity validates ending the world as we know it that any genuine form of collective happiness is precluded. Indeed, the prevalence of drugs, escapism, and mind-numbing popular music among our young is a warning that those inevitably entrusted with the future are tuning out of a world with no solidity or promise.

Yet, the challenge to postmodernity is much more than the need to overcome fragmentation and division. Wholeness, in other words, is not nearly enough. Part of our challenge has to do with rescuing the spirit. Already toward the close of the nineteenth century, Nietzsche delivered the startling message that God is dead—a message with prophetic consequences that continue to reverberate. If God is dead, then these partial identities become new absolutes, and totalizing approaches to politics and society are bound to emerge, and have. Secular religions become either redundant rubber stamps for science and the state or become demonic historical forces, with idolatrous tendencies invisibly embedded in the whole edifice of modernism. Jean-Paul Sartre epitomized the absurdity of modern existence by associating it with nausea in the face of reality. The modern circumstance is groundless in the fundamental, ultimate sense of endowing our existence with a meaning beyond our mortality. When my death means everything, the death of others means nothing. The ethos of the terrorist becomes as natural as it is disruptive in such a world. And this pertains whether those relying upon terror do so with kidnappings and hijackings, with covert operations and high technology attacks on civilian targets, or with weaponry of mass destruction. The revolutionary and the functionary, relying on violent means, tend to become mirror images of what it is they purport to deplore.

The postmodern in this broader sense implies the rediscovery of normative and spiritual ground upon which to find meaning in human existence. It does not imply a return to the past, even to the early modern or premodern reality of a world given coherence and religious sanction by the acceptance of the reign of the great monotheistic religions with their faith bestowed in a centralized, hierarchical, patriarchal deity reigning over earthly matters from a heavenly throne. The postmodern horizon of spiritual recovery proceeds on a different basis: *a dispersion of spiritual energy that is associated with the sacredness of the whole universe and a related feminization of political life that finds power in relations rather than in capabilities for dominance and destruction, in earthborne more than skyborne energy.* Unity without centralization or hierarchy provides the only firm constraint upon the design of desirable world-order arrangements for the future.

II. Two Texts

To clarify this orientation, I wish to comment upon two passages, each written by a prophetic postmodern voice. The first is taken from Martin Buber's *Paths in Utopia:*

> The vision of 'what should be'—independent though it may sometimes appear of personal will —is yet inseparable from a critical and fundamental relationship to the existing condition of humanity. All suf-

fering under a social order prepares the soul for vision and what the soul receives in this vision strengthens and deepens its insight into the perversity of what is perverted.[2]

Buber's rooting of vision in the actuality of suffering ensures that the essence of our political endeavors will be centered upon those who are most victimized by present arrangements. Unless we understand "the perversity of what is perverted," all the good will in the world cannot help. At the same time, it becomes critical not to reproduce perversity in our struggle against it; in questioning the role of violence in political life, we are reacting to the experience of betrayal that has been associated with so much revolutionary violence in our century. That is, a posture of struggle seems predicated upon perversity; but, including a critical assessment of the place of violence, not necessarily its unconditional rejection, puts a heavy burden on persuasion to set forth those exceptional, limited justifications.

The second passage is from Lewis Mumford's *The Transformations of Man:*

[T]he emergence of New World culture, in completed form, in our time has produced in itself a world crisis. As far as records tell, this is the first planet-wide crisis that has taken place since the last glacial period. But the menace that then came from nature now comes from the busy hands and minds of men.[3]

The crisis of which Mumford writes is an outcome of technology and its appropriation for modernist purposes, that is, to promote the supremacy of certain fragments at the expense of subjugating others. Such patterns in pure form produce slavery, and they are also represented in more diluted forms by the relations between the Western and non-Western world, by the relations between white peoples and peoples of color, by the relations of industrializing societies and indigenous peoples, by the relations of men and women. The result of these structures is suffering, victimization. Mumford calls our attention to the new dimension—its global-scale—and yet does so in the patriarchal, patronizing idiom of modernity, writing of humanity and personhood by reliance on the species-splitting rhetoric of "man" to denote the whole. Nuclear weaponry is both the culmination of modernism and a new circumstance suggesting that superior technology as a basis of dominance is now analogous to the once active threat of a catastrophic resurfacing of the planet by glacial formation. Nuclear winter is the sequel to the historical possibility of "glacial winter." A dramatic difference is that now we have fashioned our own jeopardy and might be in a position to overcome it, whereas with respect to glaciers, the natural forces at work were beyond our control and still are.

III. Contra Disneyland Postmodernism

The first requirement for a curative response is confidence in the future. Such confidence involves both a vision of something desirable and a willingness to risk a great deal to attain it. Without sacrifice, commitment, jeopardy, it is impossible to confront successfully a well-entrenched system of beliefs, institutions, and practices. In this regard, it is important to appreciate the resilience and continuing success of the state as a focus for political loyalty, of nationalism as a mobilizing ideology, of the market as a basis for allocating resources, of war potential as the fulcrum of international stability, and of nuclear weapons as providing the only deterrence capable of avoiding world war between East and West. We cannot achieve a postmodern reality without transforming the essential nature of these main pillars of modernism, and yet the pillars continue to be so firmly in place that they cannot be successfully challenged by direct action. This underlying situation has created a widespread condition of cultural despair, even if often unacknowledged. The failures of the United Nations and of disarmament and foreign aid efforts add to this despair, as does the general atmosphere of acrimony in international relations which has set the tone since 1945, the reliance by the superpowers on military means to uphold their global position, and the incidence of warfare and poverty in many Third World countries, especially in settings of continuing population growth.

Finding a hopeful basis for understanding and action, while accepting this difficult setting, is what we need to concentrate our mental energies upon. Among several pitfalls are various categories of false hope: the utopianism of muddling through, the utopianism of a technological fix (for example, the Strategic Defense Initiative [SDI]), the fundamentalism of an assured true path, and the fundamentalism of an unavoidable Armageddon.

The critique and the jeopardy are plainer than is a direction for response. Living amid American affluence, societal change requires nothing more than the cumulative effects of personal will, it is often claimed, at least implicitly. It is necessary to be cautious, even skeptical, about such claims. To posit a new age shift in civilization without any accompanying struggle invites a variety of misunderstandings, even deceptions.

My concern is this: There is a cultural disposition evident in certain circles, especially prominent in California, to suppose that we can complete the transition to the postmodern by taking an appropriate psychological stance without ever engaging concrete sources of resistance, including human depravity and greed. I am suspicious on these grounds of "the Aquarian conspiracy," "the Hunger Project," "Beyond War," and many other well-intentioned navigational guides premised on seductive recipes for inner work and smooth sailing. Epitomizing what I regard as misguided orientations toward the postmodern are the recent publications of the Ark Foundation, especially the two edited volumes of soft advocacy put out by Don

Carlson and Craig Comstock.[4] I cannot conceive of useful knowledge that is not somehow grounded on specifics, particularly on the dirty hands of our own governing process when it comes to such matters as the unabated legacy of destruction directed at the indigenous peoples of our own continent, the moral scandal of financing and promoting *contra* terrorism in Central America, the still unacknowledged criminality of dropping atomic bombs on Hiroshima and Nagasaki and of preparing for nuclear war, and the incredible discrepancy between our overall affluence and the growing numbers of homeless and hungry persons scattered about our cities.

My reasoning here relies on the fused insight of Buber and Mumford, in line with Gandhi, Tolstoy, Jesus, Martin Luther King, Desmond Tutu, Henry David Thoreau, and all others who insist that moral concern is serious only if it includes active participation in ongoing struggles against injustice and suffering. Such a process may reject violence as a means of struggle, or reserve it for extreme situations and limited roles, but it cannot dispense with criticism and explication of power structures or with exposure and indictment of abusive elites. The contrary soft style of peace advocacy searches obsessively for validation and encouragement from established leaders, especially former heads of state and military commanders, to demonstrate a supposedly uniform and shared commitment to rid the world of nuclear weapons, or even war. The implicit intention is to suggest that power-wielders are in good faith and share the objectives of peace-seekers, that a new world order can be brought about by inner shifts in consciousness and by mutual recognitions of good faith. No conflicts are inherent, it is assumed, and the posture of opposition or struggle is regarded as superfluous and destructive of opportunities for cooperative, curative efforts. In their eagerness for support, soft advocates often rip rhetorical flourishes of officials from the overall context of the careers, beliefs, and convictions of such leaders; frequently, peace-oriented assertions amount to rear-mirror wisdom delivered from the largely detached sanctuary of retirement from public life. Perhaps the most notorious illustration of soft advocacy is the constant reiteration of Eisenhower's warning about the military industrial complex in his farewell address. Over the years, few have paused to ask why President Eisenhower waited until retirement from public life to deliver this warning and why he did so much to conventionalize the role of nuclear weapons in the armed forces while he led the country as our most popularly elected postwar president. Rarely is it observed that those who gain access to militarized power structures cannot govern effectively unless they accept the overall legitimacy of the national security consensus, that co-option and careerism operate as potent conscience-numbing forces upon those who act prominently on behalf of modernist and highly militarized structures. It is not surprising, then, that glimmerings of conscience reemerge as individuals are released from these structures by retirement, but neither is it appropriate to regard such expressions of concern as related to prospects for change in the structures themselves.

My view is this: until we pronounce clearly upon these concrete issues of modernist illegitimacy, the quest and promise of a postmodern world is, despite all protestations, a disguised, if unwitting, expression of acceptance of the destructive character of modernity. This critical imperative entails an overall attitude of resistance, or at minimum skepticism toward the policies and proposals of established structures and elites. For these reasons, soft advocacy is to be rejected as misleading and diversionary, although its focus on shifting values and lifestyles is a helpful emphasis as is its implicit rejection of bloody revolutionary tactics. In essence, my critique comes down to an indictment of soft advocacy or Disneyland postmodernism for acting as a kind of opiate, promising an eventual salvation without any transitional unpleasantness. In some ways, this critique is analogous to Marx's indictment of religion as "the opiate of the people," having in mind the Christian message of patience for the rewards of the next world if one's lot in this life seemed demeaning or unfair.

Five distinct problematic aspects can be identified as associated with Disneyland postmodernism:

1. An abstract affirmation of a holistic, harmonious future as implicit or imminent can be an evasion of the ethical injunction to engage concretely in the struggle to overcome suffering and to help sustain the life prospects of present and future generations.

2. Some integrative dynamics move toward a homogenized, mercantile holism, which ensnares the imagination and the human spirit. Whether we conceive of the future by the aculturating music played in international hotel chains or in the manner of the Merrill Lynch bull roaming the world in search of investment bargains beneath the slogan, "Your world should know no boundaries," such a future may organize the planet globally, but it will do so with a colonizing logic. See, for example, the injunction, "Think Global," highlighted in newsprint advertizing on behalf of the Scudder Global Fund, given spatial form by a logo consisting of a global map girdled by double bands of ticker tape filled with stock quotations.

3. The tendency to reinterpret science and natural reality as confirmatory of a spiritual grounding for human endeavors is useful as a basis for healing the cultural wounds of modernism, but it is not necessarily indicative of an overall transformation of the civilizational worldview, at least not in accordance with a time-frame relevant for the solution of the main world-order challenges: war, famine, disease, oppression, environmental decay, alienation, and poverty.

4. The emphasis on holistic possibilities of encompassing conflict needs to be convincingly reconciled with the preservation and extension of diversity. Planetary ecology on any axis of concern is better served if diversity is seen as a resource that is nurtured simultaneously with an awareness of the wholeness and oneness of our identity as a species; a style of dialectical interpretation is needed to convey the interplay of wholeness and diversity as positive elements.

5. A detached imagery of postmodernism is largely an expression of the privileged status of the West, and it does not take enough serious account of the urgent preoccupations of non-Western peoples or of those who are "losers" in the West. As such, its claims have a provincial flavor, and these claims risk dismissal elsewhere as frivolous diversions.

Taking heed of these caveats enables the difficult search for political pathways to a postmodern world. This undertaking needs what Raymond Williams identifies as " . . . the difficult business of gaining confidence in our own energies and capacities. . . ."[5]

IV. A Second Axial Upheaval

Karl Jaspers, Lewis Mumford, Paul Tillich, and Elise Boulding have called our attention to an initial axial age several centuries before Jesus in which several great religions became established under diverse cultural and geographic conditions. The essence of the axial idea is a profound alteration in the shape of civilization and the content of human consciousness, and a reorientation of normative outlook and guiding values.

With the exhaustion of modernizing energies, and with the various types of normative reactions taking hold in opposition to specific forms of domination and destructive potential characteristic of the modern, it seems appropriate to conceive of the possible emergence of a second axial age. The tentativeness of this assertion arises from the difficulty of interpreting inchoate social forces and contradictory types of evidence. The time-interval of emergence is surely likely to be a matter of decades, if not considerably longer. Yet, there is something helpful about the imagery of foundational reality that is bound up with the axial notion. It is also at the basis of the postmodern possibility.

Put differently, if we are experiencing the early stages of a second axial upheaval, then this is what will enable establishment of a postmodern world. At present, the axial upheaval seems mainly an expression of oppositional imagery active at only the margins of modernism, as a kind of snapping at the heels: initiatives against violence, bureaucracy, centralizing technology, hierarchy, patriarchy, ecological carelessness. But it is also beginning to nourish some new modes of action: nonviolent practices, participatory organizations, soft-energy paths and gentle technology, democratizing politics, feminizing leadership and tactics, spiritualized nature, green consciousness. It is the mixing of these axial elements in a variety of concrete embodiments as innovative forms of social action that provides inspiration: The Green Party, Greenham Common, Ground Zero (Seattle), Lokayan, Chipko Movement, Solidarity, The Great Peace Journey. Each of these expressions of creative energy works out tensions between different pulls, given the historical setting and felt urgencies of specific conjunctures of time and space. Each initiative may wither, or succumb to mainstream modernist conventional wisdom about "winning" in "the real world." But each is worthy of study and help because it is informed by the postmodern possibility of a new axial breakthrough.

Let me be clearer: These axial gropings contrast with modernist impulses toward reform, whether initiated at the level of state action or the grassroots. Examples of modernist reform: Freeze Movement, Superpower Summits, arms control negotiations, antiapartheid struggle, law of the seas treaty, elimination of gross abuses of human rights. Each has useful, even crucial, elements which could contribute greater stability to our world, but each is dependent upon either violence or state power, or both, as the focus of its action; that is, violence or governmental initiative must be used as means and a new configuration of state power is the main image of the goal. In other words, this style of action may uncover the normative potential of modernism, and even strengthen our capacity to make the transition to the postmodern world in a relatively gentle, less abrupt manner. Nevertheless, modernist politics, however effective as a holding operation, are unable to help supersede the fragmentation, technicism, violence, and statism which ensure normative entropy and threaten us with various forms of catastrophic collapse. The implicit distinction is between holding the modern world together and transforming it for the sake of the postmodern possibility.

V. Toward a Postmodern Ethics

The ground for action in the world is a combination of normative outlook and personal identity. *The postmodern identity is constituted by a deep feeling of unity with others* (what Erik Erikson regards as *species identity) and with nature (a coevolutionary relation).* It is also constituted by a sense of *freedom and responsibility for one's own behavior,* and a *refusal to accept as unconditional the authority of any external source of truth.* These shared orientations provide a foundation for a postmodern ethics that is beginning to take shape in many distinct settings of challenge and response. Postmodern ethics has ancient roots that can be associated with the lives of Socrates, Jesus, the Buddha, even St. Francis, more in the character of an embodiment in action than an abstract precept of conduct. Some features can be identified:

1. React to the intolerable. There is room for disagreement as to individual and societal goals, but there is no reason to accept avoidable suffering and every reason to oppose deliberate efforts to inflict pain and cause suffering. The concreteness of pain and suffering (psychic humiliation as well as physical torment) provides us with an assurance that our intentions and actions are beneficial.

2. Refuse to lie or manifest mistrust. If any institution seeks obedience by insisting that lies be told, it is essential to resist even if it means confinement and pain. If a system of order implants distrust, it is essential to base personal relations on openness and truthfulness. Adam Michnik has expressed this stance of sacrificial nonviolent defiance as the basis of an ethical life in authoritarian Poland, identifying the state and the Communist Party as associated with an ethics of pervasive lying and mistrust. There is no way that an institution can deprive us of this capacity to be truthful and trusting, and as long as we are, a crucial domain of freedom is retained, however totalitarian the regime.

3. *Regard personal relations as models for the good society.* The practices of everyday life reproduce and prefigure the patterns of more complex, impersonal relations. Our sense of order and authority is expressed by the way we live our life and organize its activities at every level of social organization, starting with the family and clan. There is a close bond between desirable governance for the family and for the human family. A patriarchal social movement cannot contribute to the construction of a beneficial postmodernism.

4. *The future is now.* Within our zones of autonomous existence, we can live as if the desired future is here and, by doing, help bring the desired transformation about.

5. *The primacy of conscience.* Trusting others depends on trusting and acting upon one's own sense of right and wrong. Such attitudes encourage nonviolent, yet militant, resistance and expectations of accountability, especially by those with power. There is also a burden to adopt a critical view of what is near, within the range of ethical reach. Criticizing one's own government is an especially valuable expression of patriotism in our historical epoch, especially if carried on within an ascendent state that associates its security with superior military prowess and with the control of extraterritorial developments. This latter disposition to project power and influence strengthens the impulse toward intervention and violent encounter.

6. *Journey to the future.* Although we can model the future, we must not deceive ourselves that it is in place already. Such a pretension overlooks suffering and structures of domination and distortion and facilitates escapist flights of fancy. The unifying struggle that informs reactions to various modernist failures is to establish a nonviolent, encompassing political community that allows distinct and diverse identities to flourish, overlapping and intersecting from individual to individual and group to group. It is not a specific project as such, in the manner of promoting nuclear disarmament or democratization of a given society, but rather a perspective that animates action to a sufficient degree that over time a cumulative dynamic of transformation gathers force, and eventually displaces the old superseded order. It is not an event but a process, a sufficient shift in the ground of beliefs and values, to overcome the prevalence of the modernist mind-set—a shift that has been optimistically and probably prematurely identified as ''the silent

revolution." Interpreting the weight of new normative forms is virtually impossible, as much of what is significant seems to occur at unconscious levels of awareness, or is subject to partisan perceptions, which inflate or unduly minimize. The old order retains control over most flows of information, manipulates from a modernist mind-set, and may create an impression that the desired future is more remote than is the case. Experience with unexpected revolutions at the societal scale suggests that resentments often accumulate in latent form, creating illusions of stability, which are discarded after the unexpected eruption takes place. There is the analogous ecological resilience of living systems, which ''hide'' their deterioration until almost at the verge of collapse.

7. *Be receptive to the vibrations of feminized consciousness.* Women as primary bearers of the feminine have a creative role to play, especially given the complex interplay of unity and diversity. Long ago, Schopenhauer, despite reactionary intentions, intuited this powerful vocation of women: ''Because fundamentally women exist solely for the propagation of the race and find in this their vocation, they are altogether more involved with the species than with individuals, and in their hearts take the affairs of the species more seriously than they do those of the individual.''[6] This earthly sense of the whole provides a way of reanimating our political life.

8. *Develop the ideal of the citizen pilgrim.* The pilgrim is one who is on a journey in space and time, seeking a better country, a heavenly one.[7] There are no illusions that the present is an embodiment of what is possible. The citizen pilgrim is loyal to this quest, and is not bound by any sense of duty to carry out the destructive missions of a given territorial state to which he or she owes temporary secular allegiance.

9. *There are no messiahs.* The belief that only a charismatic presence can break the bonds of oppressive structure invites quietism and co-option. The movement makes its heroes more than heroes produce a movement. If we wait for a messiah, we wait; if we react to the challenges of present and future as responsible moral agents, as aspiring citizen pilgrims, then we act. By acting a cumulative process unfolds, leaders emerge, and new horizons of realistic aspiration present themselves.

VI. TOWARD A POSTMODERN POLITICS

This period of transition imposes particular demands on the level of political action. The quest: *nurturing the new while muting the destructive features of the old,* partially superseded, yet still prevailing, political order. It is essential to reject a polarization of choice—repudiating the old as decadent and obsolete, disregarding the new as utopian and hence irrelevant. The ongoing debate between realists and utopians implies a false either/or choice. Instead, we emphasize both/when, clarifying the province of reform and the domain or radical restructuring. At this stage, the political effort needs to be one of integration, first of all in the imagination—"Time present and time past are both perhaps contained in time future." Even our separation of modernist and postmodernist possibilities is based on a dichotomy of convenience only. The displacement of modernism invites recovery of the premodern past as well as pursuit of the postmodern future. Or, as we conceive of postmodernist possibilities, it is helpful to infuse premodern understanding and wisdom. In many respects, the premodern anticipates the postmodern more helpfully than does the modern, especially by its implicit ecological worldview, its sense of religious life as embodied in the totality of individual and social practice, and its imagery of spirituality as often genderless and as dispersed among feminine and masculine centers of energy (called gods and goddesses, or deities). The messy circumstance of action involves the implication of past and future in the present, not a sequence based on lapsed premodernism, modernism now, postmodernism later. The process of moving toward a postmodern world requires that premodernist, modernist, and postmodernist forms coexist and interpenetrate within our lives and consciousness for the indefinite future.

VII. Some Modernist Achievements

In our critical response to statism, war, and nuclearism, we tend to turn from present structures in disgust. Equally harmful is our tendency to suspend a critical demeanor because of an implicit or explicit conviction that these existing structures and their presiding elites are "the only game in town." *To be critical, yet receptive to normative opportunity, seems the appropriate political outlook.*

Modernist politics have achieved some impressive gains over the past decade which can be enumerated for purposes of illustration.

1. China has had success in bringing balance to the relationship between its population and resources through a governmentally mandated policy of limiting family size to one child in most instances. This extraordinary adjustment, achieved over the span of a single generation, was possible both because of cultural conditions (ethnic homogeneity; traditions of leadership; pride in unity and practical solutions; an orientation toward reality that can be summarized as "the Confucian advantage") and of political centralization and efficiency relative to divergent social forces in civil society. Achieving this degree of population control has contributed to the confidence of Chinese leaders to move rapidly in demilitarizing directions (the innovative solution devised for the future of Hong Kong; the willingness to find a compromise based on renunciation of violence as the basis for settling the question of Taiwan's status; partial demobilization of the armed forces—about 1,000,000; shift of production from arms to civilian goods; overall tenor of moderation).

2. India and Bangladesh have had success in achieving self-sufficiency in basic foodstuffs. Relying on modernizing agriculture, the Indian subcontinent has managed to avoid the spectre of famine despite widespread, dire prophesies of doom made as recently as the 1970s. (This success is controversial, partly because ecological side effects raise the whole question of techno-agricultural manipulation and abuse of soils and plant stocks, and partly because it is not clear whether such agricultural productivity can be long sustained.)

3. The Soviet Union, even without the benefit of democracy, seems now to be governed by a leadership that is seriously committed to achieving a breakthrough in disarmament negotiations—at least stopping the nuclear arms race and reducing, if not eliminating, the nuclear weapons dimension from East/West political conflict. Under Gorbachev, the Kremlin has taken serious unilateral initiatives (including a sustained moratorium on the test ban and the virtual adoption of U. S. official positions to circumvent negotiating obstacles) and set forth far-reaching credible proposals. At Reykjavik, in late 1986, the leaders of the superpowers appeared to have agreed for some hours on a framework of total denuclearization to unfold over the course of the next decade: 50 percent reduction in nuclear missiles and warheads during the next five years, the remaining 50 percent in the subsequent five years (including balancing and reassuring adjustments in conventional force levels and a moderating of political antagonism). The breakdown of such a promising prospect should not blind us to the significance of its occurrence. For a brief interval, at least, the leaders of the most powerful states apparently associated their security with the complete abolition of nuclear weaponry. Such a dramatic departure from security through nuclearism is something that not even the mainstream Western peace movement dared demand (consider the U. S. freeze movement or European resistance to the deployment of Pershing II/Cruise missiles). Note, also, that both superpowers endorse the moral repudiation of nuclear deterrence, the United States purporting to rely on the drastic technical fix of the SDI, while the Soviet Union is seemingly committed to fostering a disarming process.

4. Greece, New Zealand, and the Philippines have tried to limit their participation in nuclearism by challenging the prerogatives of the nuclear superpowers in specific ways. The new Aquino constitution for the Philippines had a nonnuclear provision: "The Philippines, consistent with national interest, adopts and pursues a policy of freedom from nuclear weapons in its territory." In a harsh editorial, *The Wall Street Journal* called this stance "a real time bomb" and an "ostrich policy of declaring oneself a nuclear-free zone."[8] The most explosive aspect of this issue arises from the well-known "secret" that the United States government uses its huge foreign bases in the Philippines as depots for the storage of nuclear warheads.

5. Argentina, Brazil, Uruguay, Haiti, and the Philippines have experienced transitions from dictatorial and military rule to some form of con-

stitutional order without having to go through a period of civil strife. Many democratizing movements in different countries seek to soften the relations between state and civil society, making the former responsive to the will of the latter. Ample evidence exists, despite the fragility of each of these transitions, that the militarized state cannot permanently extinguish the flames of public discontent, no matter how brutal its repressive means. Popular sovereignty is alive and well in many parts of the world, suggesting that the centralized, modern state can be challenged and reformed by nonviolent mass action.

6. Several governments, including that of Bolivia, have shown the capacity to overcome triple digit inflation. Hyper-inflation, if unabated, destroys the social fabric of modernist arrangements, inviting nihilism and fanatical political responses. To constrain inflation allows other constructive societal developments to gain strength.

7. Several governments have displayed a willingness and capacity to relinquish their reliance on hard drugs as a source of foreign exchange earnings, although the overall record of response remains mixed and inconclusive.

8. The United Nations and its large family of more specific international institutions, despite numerous difficulties, remains intact and obtains quasi-universal participation.

9. Governments have established and continuously expand cooperative frameworks of varying strength in areas of trade, money, pollution control, antiterrorism, and almost succeeded in establishing a comprehensive global framework to regulate the use of oceans.

Each of these instances of achievements have shadow sides, making assessment complex. Yet, the evidence exists that governments have room for maneuver and that popular sovereignty can successfully challenge bureaucratic power and military/paramilitary styles of rulership. Positive, modernist action remains possible, and could be strengthened by postmodernist pressures and perspectives. We do not yet reliably know the outer limit of normative potential for modernist structures, but it is essential to keep probing.

VIII. POSTMODERNIST GROPINGS

Beyond the modern, a politics is emerging with a new dimension: nonviolent, militant, feminized, transnational, grassroots, informal, and inspired by premodernist wisdom and insight. In an industrialized democracy with a functioning constitution, this emergent postmodern politics does not entrust the future to traditional forms of indirect participation: traditional parties, electoral campaigns, congressional lobbying, representative institutions, enlightened presidential leadership. The emphasis is either upon a radical reorientation of traditional vehicles (Green Party) or upon "antipolitics" (forms of collective expression that are extranormal).

A crucial organizing basis for postmodern politics is associated with social movements of varying character:

1. The new social movements. In the 1970s, a series of powerful societal initiatives was associated with movement activity: in the setting of opposition to nuclear power plants, on behalf of environmental protection, in opposition to specific weapons and deployments, on behalf of women, on behalf of sexually deviant groups, on behalf of indigenous peoples. These movements originated out of normative grievances or fears, as well as a sense of skepticism about the character of conventional political mechanisms of change and control. As these movements evolved, splits emerged paralleling the modern/postmodern divide, especially as to the relation between process and substance. Beyond renouncing violence and shifting expectations for renewal and reform away from the political center, there was significance attached to finding practical ways of organizing that did not reproduce hierarchical, patriarchal patterns.

2. Popular sovereignty ascendent. A widespread withdrawal of deference to the centralized state apparatus is found in all sectors of the world, although not in every society. The issue of legitimacy is being contested in many forms for both efficiency and normative reasons, usually expressed as demands for democratizing reforms, including procedures enabling access to governmental authority and making leaders accountable for abuses of state power, either by way of economic corruption or repression of dissenters. Each struggle has its own specific character, but the overall claims of popular sovereignty are being asserted as existential demands; these cannot be satisfied by abstractions about a fictitious social contract vesting power in the state in exchange for public order or about the inherently liberating character of postrevolutionary proletarian rule. Both liberalism and Marxism/Leninism are no longer presumed legitimate, especially by those who reject the view that nationalist or class identity of a government is the decisive test of legitimacy. The appeal of premodern politics, especially when not hidden by layers of sentimental nostalgia, is its experience with holistic patterns of practice and with minimal institutional structure.

3. Secular supremacy challenged. In many forms, religious deference to the state is also diminishing and being reversed. Secular doctrines of separation of church and state are under attack from both fundamentalist and postmodernist outlooks. The association of religious convictons and solidarity with the poor provides a ground for mass mobilization against modernist orientations toward politics. "Liberation theology" in its many varieties aspires to a reunion of secular goals and spiritual identity. Even mainstream churches are, on issues of nuclear weaponry or poverty, seeking to reclaim authority, at least to the extent of eroding the legitimacy of the state by counterposing contrasting normative imperatives that are addressed to the individual consciences of adherents. They are thereby challenging modernist assumptions that obedience and respect for the state are aspects of good citizenship.

4. Reclaiming law. Another field of postmodern political action is in relation to law. By invoking international law and personal conscience as justifications for violating domestic law, individuals and groups are calling into question unconditional notions of sovereignty and statist national security policy. Appealing to a *global normative order* suggests the importance of bonds among societies that take precedence over the state/society nexus. This postmodernist priority is emphasized by adherence to international human rights standards, and even more so by the Nuremberg Obligation that holds leaders and policymakers criminally liable for violations of international law in the war/peace area and imposes responsibility on individuals and even on citizens to implement the legal order against their own leadership; a freely elected government acquires no exemption from accountability. Another expression of this refusal any longer to regard law as belonging exclusively to the state is the establishment of judicial frameworks by informal and populist initiative: in many countries "tribunals" hear evidence, interview witnesses, render judgments on issues of public policy. There have been several tribunals dedicated to a legal assessment of reliance on nuclear weaponry under varying conditions, on controversial uses of military force (e.g., Vietnam, Afghanistan, Nicaragua), on denials of human rights (e.g., South Africa, Philippines under Marcos). This process of informal adjudication has been given institutional expression in the Permanent Peoples Tribunal (a project of the Rome-based International League for the Rights of Peoples), which carries out its assessment of public wrongs in relation to its own constitutional document—the Algiers Declaration of the Rights of Peoples.

5. Transnational relief. Rock concerts for overseas famine and disasters have created a new idiom for helping acute victims of calamity. Such events tend to be multiracial, multiethnic, multinational in character and create psychological bonds of solidarity that circumvent normal diplomatic channels and are not at all delimited by territorial boundaries.

6. Transnational information. The distrust of state motives, plus the general tendency to confuse information with propaganda, has generated distrust of official sources. It was established late in 1986 that intelligence agencies of the U.S. government had intensified the war between Iran and Iraq by a deliberate campaign of disinformation; a few months earlier a similar campaign was uncovered designed to portray Qadaffi as an archterrorist, evidently to build public support for punitive violence against Libya. Our expectations of government have fallen so low that we tend to accept such disclosures as "routine" and fault leaders not for what they did but for their failure to come clean or step forward with a ritual apology. In reality, the distortions that are part of this geopolitical power game—the negative pole of modernist politics—are quite lethal in their impact on life and community, either by building a false case for military force (as with Libya) or through encouraging hostile misperception (as with Iran and Iraq).

In view of this statist tendency to distort information, private associations with small resources but high integrity can help reshape public debate and perceptions. Amnesty International in the human rights area and Swedish International Peace Research Institute are two instances of successful efforts to provide generally reliable information in settings where partisan passions frequently distort or obscure.

IX. CONCLUSION

The promise of a postmodern world depends on human initiative, as well as upon historical tendencies. The prefiguring of the future in our imaginations and lives gives each of us the possibility and also a responsibility to act, but not merely by a leap in time. It depends on bringing postmodern ethics and politics concretely to bear as therapy for the wounds which bring so much pain to those with whom we share the planet. Taking suffering seriously is the best indication that we care about the future in a way that matters.

Martin Luther King once told his congregation at the Ebenezar Baptist Church in Atlanta that "dissent and nonconformity were the essence of true Christianity."[9] I am inclined to emphasize dissent and nonconformity as equally indispensable for an authentic embrace of the postmodern possibility. Unless we link our bodies and resources to the various struggles against the specific crimes of modernity, we are not ethically or politically fit to cross that great divide linking present to future. Contrariwise, if we become immersed totally in antimodernist projects, however valuable, we lose contact with the most powerful set of liberating energies at work in our personal and public lives during this historical epoch. *To be postmodern, we need to develop the practices and nurture the consciousness* that simultaneously inhabits premodern, modern, and postmodern realms of actual and potential being.

NOTES

1. Raymond Williams, *The Year 2000* (New York: Pantheon, 1983), 26.

2. Martin Buber, *Paths in Utopia* (London: Routledge & Kegan Paul, 1949), 7.

3. Lewis Mumford, *The Transformations of Man* (New York: Harper & Row, 1956), 95.

4. The two titles edited by Don Carlson and Craig Comstock are *Citizen Summitry* and *Securing Our Planet*, both published in 1986 by Jeremy P. Tarcher and distributed by St. Martin's Press.

5. Raymond Williams, *The Year 2000*, 268.

6. Arthur Schopenhauer, *Essays and Aphorisms* (New York: Penguin, 1970), 84.

7. *The Bible: The Letter to the Hebrews* 11:13–16.

8. "The Philippines Constitution," *Wall Street Journal,* January 4, 1987.

9. Quoted in D. Garrow, *Bearing the Cross* (New York: Morrow, 1986), 459. This essay was originally prepared for a conference held January 16–20, 1987, which spanned Martin Luther King, Jr., weekend.

6

POSTMODERN
SOCIAL POLICY

John B. Cobb, Jr.

Social policy reflects social theory. The feature of social theory to which I address these brief remarks is the relation of the individual to society. I want first, in caricature fashion, to state what I see as the characteristic form of modern social theory on this point, then to contrast the implications of a postmodern vision, and finally, to comment on policy implications.

Much of modern social thought reflects the seventeenth-century theory of the social compact. This theory adopts the myth of a state of nature in which each individual or household was independent of all the others. In the Hobbesian version, this meant a war of each against all, a condition which entailed misery for all. For this reason, it was in the best interest of all to surrender their freedom to a single ruler who could guarantee the order needed for survival. Thus, the nation-state, with absolute power, is the logical result of the human condition.

The more popular and influential Lockean version pictured the state of nature less balefully. Nevertheless, individuals still found turning over certain portions of their freedom and rights to a centralized government in exchange for the protection of their property to their advantage. In this case, too, attention is focused on the individual and the nation-state as the two major units of social reality.

The modern period is the age of nationalism. Nations have differed as to whether they have granted and enforced the rights of individuals or sacrificed them to the maximization of state power, but either way individual and nation have been the primary foci. Of course, there have been other social groupings, and many of these have been studied by sociologists, but they have been subordinated to these two foci. There is a tendency to view these other societies in terms of the rights of individuals to enter voluntary associations, rights that are granted or withheld by the state.

Viewed from without, Marxist nations appear to illustrate this general thesis well. They seem to be totalitarian states with little regard for human rights and therefore intolerant of social groupings not controlled by the state. But Marxist *theory* does offer an alternative to nationalism. It holds that the determinant societies consist in classes rather than nation-states. National governments are functions of dominant economic classes. People are first and foremost members of the proletariat or the bourgeoise and only secondarily French or German.

Thus far, the evidence does not support this Marxist thesis. The French proletariat fought the German proletariat when France went to war with Germany. It might be supposed that this was because of the coercive power of the nation-state to force its citizens to fight for it. But this account has only limited explanatory power. On the whole, French and German workers voluntarily made sacrifices for the sake of their nations in order to defeat one another.

The undoubted importance of nation-states has led "realists" to view them as agents in the international scene, each seeking its interests in terms of power and wealth. The theories developed on the basis of this hypostatization of nation-states frequently accord well with what actually happens among them. Hence, modern theory is reenforced. Nevertheless, this is at best a gross simplification of the social reality. To gain a critical perspective on nationalism, we will examine it more closely.

Nationalism has two major features: First, it selects a particular level from the hierarchy of political organization and locates full sovereignty there. Second, it seeks to subordinate all other social groupings and loyalties to the nation.

With respect to the first of these two features, nationalism is best contrasted with feudalism, especially because it arose in opposition to that other system. Feudal society was organized hierarchically. The peasant and soldier owed loyalty to the local feudal lord who in turn owed loyalty to a higher lord and so forth, ideally to the level of the emperor of all of Christendom. But fealty did not entail sheer submission. There were duties and obligations down as well as up the hierarchy. No one level stood out as all-important. Nations arose as rejections of any higher authority, such as the Holy Roman Empire, and as means of subordinating all lower ones, the feudal aristocracy. Nationalism as an ideology supported this move.

Of course, nationalism has never wholly triumphed in this goal. Local and regional loyalties remain strong, and many people have a sense of belonging to the wider society of humanity as well as to a particular nation. Difficulties are especially acute where national boundaries do not correspond to ethnic, linguistic, and religious ones. This lack of correspondence has occurred where nations have been created by international treaties or have arisen out of former European colonies whose boundaries were imposed by conquest from without rather than by organic development from within. Nevertheless, people can act politically on the global scene only through nation-states. Nongovernmental organizations can try to influence the decisions of the United Nations, for example, but they cannot participate directly in its deliberations.

Nationalism also sought to concentrate power in the state, thereby subordinating all other societies to the political one. At this point, however, nations have never been fully successful, and contemporary ideology generally rejects this goal. Almost all national constitutions allow citizens rights of assemblage, which permit participation in societies that cross national boundaries and that cannot be completely controlled by the state.

Catholic nations have always been forced to compromise their nationalism by recognizing some power over religious institutions on the part of the Vatican. Protestant nations nationalized the churches in an effort to assert national authority, but they were forced to give some autonomy even to the national churches, and they have also been compelled to tolerate independent churches. Since the Enlightenment, many other forms of cultural, humanitarian, educational, scientific, and even political association have come into being that do not acknowledge national control. The tension between nationalism and these nonnational societies is always latent and from time to time becomes acute. Today, China seeks to offer religious freedom to its people, but it refuses to recognize the authority of the pope.

We have noted that the easiest way for the modern theory to express this problem is in terms of the rights of individuals. Because it acknowledges the full reality of individuals as well as states, the tension between individual rights and state sovereignty can be readily comprehended. The difference between incorporation in the national society and participation in a religious society is often viewed in terms of the distinction between necessary and voluntary associations: one belongs to a nation by necessity of birth, while one has the *right* to associate voluntarily with other like-minded individuals.

These brief remarks should suffice to indicate that the reality of social life does not correspond perfectly to modern theory even in the modern period. Nationalism is a contingent historical phenomenon, not the necessary or inevitable organization of social life. Also, commitment to the ideology that supports it is closely related to the modern worldview. That worldview sees reality composed of self-contained and mutually external individual entities. Society is, therefore, a matter of association among such individuals. The assumption has been that association in nation-states was necessary, other associations, voluntary. The nation-states, thus, have become *given* entities for further theoretical reflection, and have been treated as substantial entities in their own right, whereas other associations are studied more as products of the exercise of individual freedom. The messy reality in which each person is simultaneously a part of many societies with vague and fluctuating boundaries does not fit the modern vision.

Consider what happens if we shift to a postmodern image of the relation of individuals to society. In this case, we reject the individualism that underlies the myth of the state of nature: persons are social products through and through. At the same time, we deny that societies are rightly seen as individuals: they are not agents; all agency and all value are located in the individuals. A nation is nothing but the individuals who comprise it, and those individuals are social beings in their very constitution.

But note that the social constitution of individuals does not mean that the nation is the only society, or even the major society, which constitutes them. In a primal society, in which a tribe is considered a nation, this simple case may be approximated. That is, the individual is constituted by participation in the life of the tribe, because the tribe is at once the cultural society, the linguistic society, the religious society, the economic society, and the educational society. The distinctions implied in such a list simply have no meaning in that setting. One may say symmetrically that the tribe consists in its individual members and that the individual members are tribal beings.

Today, as already noted, most individuals are constituted by membership in *many* societies. I am not only a citizen of the United States but also a member of the United Methodist Church, a professor, a Democrat, an environmentalist, and so forth. Also, each of these designations involves a selection of only one level of a set of levels of which it is a member. I am a citizen of Claremont, a Californian, and a North American as well as a citizen of the United States. I am a member of a local congregation and an Annual Conference as well as of the United Methodist Church, and more important than my identity as a United Methodist is my identity as a Christian. Even such listings give the impression that societies are more clearly defined and delimited than is the case.

The modern distinction between the necessary and the voluntary societies to which one belongs clearly has its usefulness, but from a postmodern point of view it is exaggerated. There are voluntary and involuntary elements in all forms of belonging. Even though one is born into a certain cultural-linguistic society, one can choose to identify strongly with it or to disidentify to a considerable degree. This is not a once-and-for-all choice but one made repeatedly in subtle ways. At the other extreme, when I became an environmentalist, the voluntary element was prominent, but it is an exaggeration to say that I chose to become an environmentalist. On the contrary, as I became aware of the situation in new ways, I discovered that I had become an environmentalist. I began to feel a kinship with persons whose concerns I had not previously understood and to be inwardly shaped by relating with them.

An analysis of this sort leads to the conclusion that there are no substantial units of which society is composed. Nations do not have the kind of existence attributed to them in much modern theory and neither does any other form of society. Yet societies are immensely important. To understand how they shape the agency of individuals, so that most human behavior expresses the social character of the individual, is essential to understanding the reality.

Two additional features of the postmodern view require statement here: First, the societies in which human beings participate are not composed only of human beings. No feature of modern social theory has been more damaging than this limitation. We are deeply related to our physical environment including especially the living creatures who comprise it. The "land" is not simply the backdrop against which history is enacted. We belong to the land and have no existence apart from it. The biosphere is a crucially important society for us.

Second, although we are products of societies, including the nonhuman one, we are not *merely* products. Just how we constitute ourselves out of the many societies to which we belong, just what weight we give to each, just what new synthesis we achieve out of the complexity of influences upon us, all of this is finally decided by ourselves, individually, moment by moment. Changes in societies change the individual members, but these changes can be initiated by subtle novelties in just these individual members. Freedom and creativity are real. Here are found the locus of real religion and morality and the justification for the cherishing of personal freedom.

What effect would this mode of understanding have on social policy? I have asked this question especially in relation to economic policy. There it is clear that the changes would need to be drastic. Because present policy follows from a theory of the absoluteness of individuals or individual households, it encourages policies that require the constant movement of individuals from one place to another. It pictures the individuals as consumers of goods and services and gives no value to their interrelatedness one with another. Hence, it encourages policies that produce goods for consumption at the expense of destroying established social patterns. Because economic theory treats the physical world as an inexhaustible resource for human consumption and an inexhaustible repository for human wastes, it is not surprising that economic policies lead to exhaustion of resources, increasing pollution, and profoundly inhumane treatment of other sentient beings.

The new economic policies which are needed would be *economics for community*. The question would be how to organize the economy so as to strengthen ties with the land, among workers, and among neighbors. Instead of a primarily global economy, we would seek to develop bioregional economies which are sustainable in relation to the land and allow for maximum participation by all those involved.

Such a move would involve political policies as well. Currently, the movement to a global economy has brought into being immensely powerful forces that cannot be controlled by nation-states. The relativization of national power is healthy. But the subordination of nations to special economic interests is not healthy. It removes power still further from those who are controlled by it. The vast majority of people now have virtually no influence on the decisions that determine most of what happens to them. These decisions also largely deny the community between humanity and the land. The movement to a bioregional economy would call for a different relativization of national power. Bioregions may sometimes cross national boundaries or include several countries. At other times, they may be sections of a single country. In any case, the development of economy along those lines will require structures of political power that support this development.

But human beings are not only economic beings; we are members of other societies as well. Many of these are not local or geographical. *Politics for community* will encourage and strengthen these societies as well. Often these communities will consist of persons from many parts of the world. Hence, they will complement and check the regionalism engendered by bioregional economics, while both work together to weaken the nationalism of the modern period.

The postmodern accent in the evaluation of societies is participation. *Community is in fact society in which participation is realized.* Of course, participation is always a matter of degree. The term *society* puts the accent on the way the individual is constituted by the influences of others. The term *community* accents the extent to which the decisions made by individuals can be taken up by the other members of the society, at least for consideration. Such participation in community is possible only where individuals transcend social formation. *Community* presupposes the element of freedom in the members of the society and gives that freedom a positive role. This positive role requires economic, political, and other social structures that encourage freedom, personal expression, and ways in which individual contributions can be appropriated by others. *Social policy should recognize the given importance of society and go on to encourage community in this full sense.* This principle means that the body politic should commit itself to providing useful work for all its members, that workers should be given a major voice in the decisions affecting their lives, that geographical regions should have power to shape the economic development within them according to the needs of the people, and so forth. Politically, the principle that social policy should encourage community means that power should be located closer to people whenever possible. It also means that, in the many other associations of which we are members, continual vigilance is needed to ensure that new voices are heard as they arise and that structures are subject to continual revision to ensure real participation on the part of as many members as possible.

In this postmodern social policy, the theme of participation will play a larger role than that of justice. Although in Biblical times, *justice* was not bound to individualistic modes of thought, this connection has been so strongly cemented in recent centuries that it will be better to let the term rest for a while. Too often, concern for justice leads to a focus on individual rights and distribution of goods within a system that is destructive of community without challenging the system itself. When more basic social change seeks justice, too often it is concerned with a rather abstract equality imposed from above. Stressing participation more than justice does not mean that justice is unimportant. Instead, the point is that the goals envisioned in the appeal for justice will be better implemented as people have a chance to take part in the decisions governing their lives. The focus on participation, however, accents their empowerment to seek what is important to them rather than what seems just to the observer.

Finally, a postmodern social theory will point to the importance of *global coordination* of the innumerable patterns of society which are jointly constitutive of individuals. The whole planet needs to be accented as constituting the inclusive community, which demands our loyalties and to which we can contribute. This accentuation would entail a further relativization of the nation-state. Global coordination of the many diverse societies would require participation by nongovernmental organizations as well as nation-states. It would require considerably more economic, political, and military power than is now at the disposal of the United Nations. But it would not entail assuming functions that can be performed by global nongovernmental agencies or by regional political ones. It would not be a transfer of the excessive power of the present nation-states to a world government. The key word is *coordination*. Just as (in the postmodern vision) the genuine benefit of one individual normally benefits those with whom that one is in community, so also at the global level the genuine benefit of one region or international institution should be to the benefit of the others. The function of coordination is to make this mutuality both real and visible so that the deep-seated vision of universal competition, so characteristic of the modern world, will be replaced by an equally powerful vision of mutuality or synergy.

Perhaps the most concrete feature of a social policy has to do with habitat. How we construct our cities is both cause and result of other aspects of our understanding of society. In the Los Angeles basin, the dominance of individualism is easy to see. The landscape is dominated by private homes and by private cars, often carrying only one person. The result, of course, is that thousands of acres of once-fertile soil have been paved over, that hundreds of thousands of people spend hours every day fighting freeway traffic, that local community is minimal, and that the air we breathe is polluted. In addition, the level of per capita consumption necessary to maintain this society is not sustainable.

How would we conceive habitat in a postmodern world? Cities would be built to occupy a minimum of arable land. They would be organized to encourage human interchange within them. They would seek to maximize the beauty both of nature and of the architecture that would be experienced by their citizens. They would minimize the time and expense devoted to transportation. They would take advantage of their surroundings and especially of the sun so as to be as independent and frugal as possible in their basic economy.

I know of only one person who has given effective concrete expression to the implementation of such a postmodern vision: Paolo Soleri. His arcologies would accomplish all these goals of a postmodern vision. For myself, I cannot envision a postmodern social policy that would not include the gradual transformation of current urban sprawl into habitat of the sort that Soleri proposes.

7

THE STEADY-STATE ECONOMY: POSTMODERN ALTERNATIVE TO GROWTHMANIA

Herman E. Daly

The economic side of life—the production, distribution, and consumption of goods—is usually placed at the opposite end of the spectrum from the spiritual. Economics is thought to deal with things material, religion with things spiritual, and the two realms supposedly do not overlap. This view, however common it may be, is very superficial. It is certainly erroneous with regard to Christianity, which emphasizes not only God's creation of the world but also God's incarnation in the world; and Christianity is by no means alone in that twofold affirmation. Although we are spiritual beings, we are nevertheless not angels. "No phosphorous, no thought," said Frederick Soddy. We could add: no prayer, no hymns, no meditation, no visions—no spiritual life at all. This point has been emphasized by modern thought.

But lest we leap illogically from this truth to the conclusion that thought is wholly determined by phosphorous, or the material world as a whole, let us remember the equally important fact, central to postmodern thought, that spiritual values are themselves causative in the material world. Spiritual values become incarnate in the material world through our actions, both purposeful and unthinking. For example, agronomist Wes Jackson says that our major crops now all have Chicago Board of Trade genes. "In other words," he says, "there are ensembles of genes in our major crops that would not be there in their particular constellation were there not a Chicago Board of Trade. . . . Our values arrange the molecules of heredity themselves." [1]

The material and the spiritual interpenetrate: the spiritual is incarnated, the material is hallowed. Economics is really about that interpenetration. Are our highest values being incarnated first, or is their place usurped by lower values? Are all materials equally capable of serving as vessels of spiritual values? Are we squandering potentially hallowable material for trivial uses? Are all values expressable as individual wants, or does the community give rise to an order of value not reducible to individual wants? How should future values be balanced against present values? How should the pleasure and pain of nonhuman creatures be reflected in the human economy?

Modern economic theory, with its single-minded pursuit of economic growth, does not allow these questions to be asked. A postmodern alternative to this "growthmania," a steady-state economy, offers no definitive answers to these questions, but it at least provides a context in which they are allowed to arise.

I. WHAT IS A STEADY-STATE ECONOMY?

A steady-state econony (SSE) is an economy with constant stocks of artifacts and people. These two populations (artifacts and people) are constant but not static. People die and artifacts depreciate. Births must replace deaths and production must replace depreciation. These *input* and *output* rates are to be equal at low levels, so that life expectancy of people and durability of artifacts will be high. Because the input flow of matter-energy equals the output flow when both populations are constant, the two flows may be merged into the concept of *throughput*. The throughput flow begins with depletion, followed by production, depreciation, and finally pollution as the wastes are returned to the environment. The economy maintains itself by this throughput in the same way that an organism maintains itself by its metabolic flow. Both economies and organisms must live by sucking low-entropy matter-energy (raw materials) from the environment and expelling high-entropy matter-energy back to the environment. [2] In an SSE, this throughput must be limited in scale to be within the regenerative and assimilative capacities of the ecosystem, in so far as possible.

It is important to be clear about what is *not* constant in an SSE. Knowledge and technology are not held constant. Neither is the distribution of income nor the allocation of resources. The SSE can develop qualitatively but does not grow in quantitative scale, just as planet earth, of which the economy is a subsystem, develops without growing. Neoclassical growth models notwithstanding, the surface of the earth does not grow at a rate equal to the rate of interest! Neither can the physical stocks and flows comprising the economy continue for long to grow at compound interest. As Nobel laureate chemist and underground economist Frederick Soddy noted long ago: "You cannot permanently pit an absurd human convention, such as the spontaneous increment of debt [compound interest], against the natural law of the spontaneous decrement of wealth [entropy]."[3]

The concept of an SSE might be further elucidated by analogy to a steady-state library, an idea that has attracted the attention of some librarians who realize that their stock of books cannot continue to grow exponentially. A steady-state library would have a constant stock of books, and whenever a new book is added an old one must be discarded. The rule would be to add a book only if it were qualitatively better than some other book whose place it would take. The steady-state library would continue to improve qualitatively, but its quantitative physical scale would remain constant. Likewise for a steady-state economy. The end of physical accretion is not the end of progress. It is more a precondition for future progress, in the sense of qualitative improvement.

One might object to the above on the grounds that conventional economic growth is not defined in physical units, but in terms of GNP, which is in units of value, not tons of steel or barrels of oil. It is quite true that GNP is in value units, because this is necessary to aggregate diverse physical units by means of a common denominator that bears some relation to the degree to which diverse things are wanted. Nevertheless a dollar's worth of GNP, just like a dollar's worth of gasoline or wheat, is an index of physical quantities. In calculating growth in real GNP, economists correct for price changes in order to capture only changes in quantity. It is also true that GNP includes services, which are not physical things. But a service is always rendered by something physical, either a skilled person or a capital good, over some time period. Growth in the service sector does not at all escape physical constraints. In any case, the SSE is defined in physical terms, *not* as zero growth in GNP.

II. WHAT IS GROWTHMANIA?

The above definition of an SSE stands in great contrast to the regime of economic growthmania characteristic of the modern world. Economic growth is currently the major goal of both capitalist and socialist countries and, of course, of third world countries. Population growth is no longer a major goal for most countries and, in fact, a slowing of demographic growth is frequently urged (in spite of considerable retrogression on this issue by the Reagan Administration). But the usual reason for urging slower demographic growth is to make room for faster economic growth. Economic growth is held to be the cure for poverty, unemployment, debt repayment, inflation, balance-of-payment deficits, pollution, depletion, the population explosion, crime, divorce, and drug addiction. In short, economic growth is both the panacea and the *summum bonum*. This is growthmania. When we add to GNP the costs of defending ourselves against the unwanted consequences of growth and happily count that as further growth, we then have hyper-growthmania. When we deplete geological capital and ecological life-support systems and count that depletion as net current income, we arrive at our present state of terminal hyper-growthmania.

World leaders seek growth above all else. Therefore to oppose growth, to advocate an SSE, is not something to be done insouciantly. One must present good reasons for believing that the growth economy will fail, and also offer good reasons for believing that an SSE will work. This is the aim of the remainder of this essay.

III. ORIGINS OF THE GROWTH DOGMA

How did we come to believe so strongly in the dogma of economic growth? What vision of the world underlies this commitment to continuous expansion, and where does it go wrong?

Open any standard introductory text in economics and in the first chapters you will find a circular flow diagram. In this diagram, exhange-value embodied in goods and services flows from firms to households and is called *national product*, while an equal flow of exchange-value embodied in factors of production returns from households to firms and is called *national income*. The picture is that of an isolated system. There are no in-flow or outflows connecting the circular flow to its ''other,'' the environment.

If we think only in terms of abstract exchange-value, the picture is reasonable. If we think in terms of money, the physical token of exchange-value, the picture is not unreasonable, but is no longer strictly correct because, although money flows in a circle, on each circuit it wears out a bit. New money must be minted or printed to make up for worn-out money. A physical throughput is thus associated with this circulation of currency. Yet, we may argue that with money the circular flow is dominant and the throughput is incidental. But when we shift to real goods and services comprising national income, the real physical processes of production and consumption, then the throughput is dominant and the circular flow is incidental. Yet, we find leading textbooks proclaiming that ''the flow of output is circular, self-renewing, and self-feeding'' and that ''the outputs of the system are returned as fresh inputs?''[4] One wonders what *fresh* could possibly mean in this context of an isolated circular flow. The authors were trying to explain the way the circular flow is replenished so it can go on for another round. But in an isolated system replenishment must be internal.

A self-replenishing isolated system is a perpetual motion machine! Replenishment requires a throughput. Abstract exchange-value may circulate in an isolated system because it has no physical dimension. Money may be thought of as flowing in a circle even though some throughput is required. But real production and consumption are in no way circular. They are based on a linear throughput beginning with depletion and ending with pollution. An economy is an open system, not an isolated system. Connections to the larger environment cannot be abstracted from without losing the most essential fact.

In the circular-flow vision, matter is arranged in production, disarranged in consumption, rearranged again in production, and so on. Nothing is ever depleted. The first law of thermodynamics can be appealed to in support of this vision: matter can be neither created nor destroyed, only rearranged. Economic growth is just a matter of accelerating the circular flow, and if nothing is used up there are no limits to growth, there is no problem of replenishment from the outside.

Of course, this picture flatly contradicts the second law of thermodynamics, which says, in effect, that the capacity to rearrange indestructible building blocks is not itself indestructible. It gets used up irrevocably. As we have seen, the standard vision sees the economy as a perpetual motion machine.

The gravity of such a contradiction for any theory is indicated by Sir Arthur Eddington:

> The law that entropy increases—the Second Law of Thermodynamics—holds, I think, the supreme position among the laws of nature. If someone points out to you that your pet theory of the universe is in disagreement with Maxwell's equations—then so much the worse for Maxwell's equations. If it is found to be contradicted by observation—well, these experimentalists do bungle things sometimes. But if your theory is found to be against the Second Law of Thermodynamics, I can give you no hope; there is nothing for it but to collapse in deepest humiliation.[5]

Economists, however, are not without some excuse for their predicament. They do not really deny that raw materials come from the environment, or that waste returns to the environment. But economic theory developed at a time when the environment was considered an infinite source and sink because it was so large relative to the economy. Because the throughput flow went from an infinite source to an infinite sink, it involved no scarcity, and could, presumably, be abstracted from for purposes of economic theory. But economic growth means that the scale of the economy gets bigger, and it is now no longer reasonable to treat it as infinitesimal relative to the ecosystem. It is time for the concept of throughput to displace the circular flow from the center stage of economic theory.[6]

If such a restructuring of economic theory is to be avoided, then the assumption of infinite sources and sinks must be in some way maintained, or else a substitute premise with similar logical consequences must be found. The latter strategy has been more common and consists in discovery of an "ultimate resource," which is both infinite in amount and infinitely substitutable for other resources and therefore has the same limits-abolishing effect as the original premise of infinite sources and sinks for physical resources. This "unlimited resource" is variously referred to as *technology, information, knowledge,* or the *human mind.* Anyone who asserts the existence of limits is soon presented with a whole litany of things that someone once said could never be done but subsequently were done. Certainly, it is dangerous business to specify limits to knowledge, but it is equally dangerous to presuppose that the content of new knowledge will abolish old limits faster than it discovers new ones. The discovery of uranium was new knowledge that increased our resource base. The subsequent discovery of the dangers of radioactivity did not further expand the resource base, but contracted it. Before getting carried away with the idea that the human mind is an "ultimate resource" generating endless growth, we must remember that, while certainly not reducible to physical or mechanical terms, the mind is not independent of the physical body. "No phosphorous, no thought," as Frederick Soddy put it. Or as Loren Eiseley reminds us, "The human mind, so frail, so perishable, so full of inexhaustible dreams and hungers, burns by the power of a leaf." Minds capable of such insight ought to be capable of showing more restraint toward leaves and phosphorous than is usually exhibited by our growth-bound economy. Mere knowledge means little to the economic system unless it is embodied in physical structures. As Kenneth Boulding reminds us, capital is knowledge imprinted on the physical world in the form of improbable arrangements.[7] But knowledge cannot be imprinted on any kind of matter by any kind of energy. The constricted entry point of knowledge into the physical economy is through the availability of low-entropy resources. No low-entropy resources, no capital—regardless of knowledge—unless the second law of thermodynamics is abolished.

It has been said that the best measure of scientists' influence is how long they can delay progress in their own disciplines. By this measure, the editors of the major economics journals are probably the most influential scientists of all time! Continuing to study economies only in terms of the circular-flow model is like studying organisms only in terms of the circulatory system, without ever mentioning the digestive tract. Yet that is what the mainline professional journals, in their dogmatic commitment to growth, insist on.

IV. MONEY FETISHISM

Money fetishism is a particular case of what Alfred North Whitehead called the "fallacy of misplaced concreteness," which consists in reasoning at one level of abstraction but applying the conclusions of that reasoning to a different level of abstraction. It is to argue that, because abstract exchange-value flows in a circle, so does real GNP; or that, because money can grow forever at compound interest, so can real wealth. What is true for the abstract symbol or token of wealth is held to be true for concrete wealth itself. This is money fetishism.

Marx, and Aristotle before him, pointed out that the danger of money fetishism arises when society shifts its focus from use-value to exchange-value. Simple commodity production, the sequence of C-M-C' (commodity-money-other commodity) begins and ends with a concrete use-value embodied in a commodity. Money is merely an intermediary facilitating exchange, the object of which is to acquire an increased use-value. C' has a greater use-value than C, but both are limited by their specific purposes. One has, say, greater need for a hammer than for a knife, but no need for two hammers, much less for fifty. As simple commodity production gave way to capitalist circulation, the sequence shifted to M-C-M' (money-commodity-more money). The sequence begins and ends with money capital, and the commodity or use-value is an intermediary step in bringing about the expansion of exchange-value. M' is greater than M, representing growth in abstract exchange-value, which does not impose its own concrete limits. One dollar of exchange-value is not as good as $2, and $50 is better still, and $1 million is much better. Unlike concrete use-values, which spoil or deteriorate when hoarded (due to entropy), abstract exchange-value can accumulate indefinitely without spoilage or storage cost. In fact, exchange-value grows by itself; it earns interest. But as Soddy told us, we cannot permanently pit an absurd human convention against a law of nature. The physical limit to growth at the micro level imposed by the absurdity of accumulating use-values has been bypassed by accumulating exchange-value (money and interest-bearing debt). Unless the aggregate of real concrete wealth can grow as fast as the accumulations of abstract exchange-value, however, there will be a devaluation of exchange-value (inflation) or some other form of debt repudiation or confiscation in order to bring accumulations of exchange-value back into equality with accumulations of real wealth.

Money fetishism and growthmania are alive and well in a world in which banks in wealthy countries make loans to poorer countries and then, when the debtor countries cannot make the repayment, the banks simply make new loans to enable the repayment of interest on old loans and thereby avoid taking a loss on a bad debt. The exponential snowballing of the debt which results when new loans are needed to pay interest on old loans cannot continue. The faith is that somehow real growth in the debtor countries will also snowball. The international debt crisis is a clear symptom of the basic disease of growthmania. Too many accumulations of money are seeking ways to grow exponentially in a world in which the physical scale of the economy is already so large relative to the ecosystem that there is not much room for exponential growth of anything having a physical dimension.

The paper economy offers more scope for "growth" than the real economy. Mergers, takeovers, "greenmail," tax avoidance schemes, and other forms of rent seeking seem more profitable than production of commodities. Accountants, investment brokers, and tax lawyers make more money than engineers because manipulating abstract symbols is easier than rearranging concrete materials into more useful structures. M-M' replaces M-C-M' Commodity use-values disappear altogether and with them all natural limits to the expansion of exchange-value.

V. LIMITS TO GROWTH: BIOPHYSICAL AND ETHICOSOCIAL

Biophysical conditions limit the possibility of economic growth even in cases where growth may still be desirable. Ethicosocial conditions limit the desirability of growth even in cases where growth is still possible.

Three interrelated conditions—finitude, entropy, and complex ecological interdependence—combine to provide the biophysical limits to growth. The growth of the economic subsystem is limited by the finite size of the total ecosystem, by its dependence on the total system as a source for low-entropy inputs and a sink for high-entropy waste outputs, and by the intricate ecological connections which are more pervasively disrupted as the physical scale of the economic subsystem grows relative to the enveloping ecosystem. Moreover, these three limits interact. Finitude would not be so limiting if everything could be recycled, but entropy prevents complete recycling of matter and forbids any recycling of energy. The entropy law would not be so limiting if environmental sources of low entropy and sinks for high entropy were infinite, but both are finite. The fact that both sources and sinks are finite, in conjunction with the entropy law, means that the ordered structures of the economic subsystem are maintained at the expense of creating a more-than-offsetting amount of disorder in the rest of the system. If the part of the system that pays the entropy bill is the sun (as in traditional peasant economies), then we need not worry. But if the disorder is imposed mainly on parts of the terrestrial ecosystem (as in modern industrial economies), than we need to count the cost of that disorder.

This disordering of the ecosystem (depletion and pollution) interferes with the life-support services rendered to the economy of other species and by natural biogeochemical cycles. The loss of these services should surely be counted as a cost of growth to be weighed against benefits at the margin. But, as we have already seen, our national accounts do not do this. Indeed, we now count the extra economic activity made necessary by the loss of free natural services as further growth! If the source of our drinking water becomes polluted, then we need more purification plants, and up goes GNP.

Even when growth is still biophysically possible, other factors may limit its desirability. Four ethicosocial propositions limiting the desirability of growth are considered below.

1. The desirability of growth financed by drawdown of geological and ecological capital is limited by the opportunity-cost imposed on future generations. Because future people cannot bid in present markets, we cannot reasonably expect current resource prices to reflect opportunity-costs beyond ten or fifteen years in the future.

2. The desirability of growth financed by takeover of the habitats of other species is limited by the extinction or reduction in number of sentient subhuman species whose habitat disappears. The loss of natural services rendered by these species (their instrumental value to us) was considered under the heading of biophysical limits. The issue here is the intrinsic value of these species as centers of sentience and creatures of God. It is not suggested that subhuman species' "utility" should count equally with that of humans, even if it were possible for these creatures to bid in the market place. But surely their feelings of pleasure and pain deserve a weight greater than *zero* in our cost-benefit analyses! Even Jeremy Bentham, from whom economists took their utilitarian philosophy, was of this opinion.

3. The desirability of aggregate growth is limited by its self-cancelling effects on individual welfare. Growth in rich countries is, at the current margin, dedicated to the satisfaction of relative rather than absolute wants. Welfare increments are more a function of changes in relative position than of absolute level of consumption. In contemplating further growth above some level of absolute income, we must agree with J. S. Mill: "Men do not desire to be rich, but to be richer than other men." Aggregate growth cannot possibly make all people richer than other people! Relative improvement is a zero-sum game in the aggregate.

4. The desirability of growth is limited by the corrosive effects on moral capital of the very attitudes that foster growth, such as glorification of both self-interest and the technocratic-reductionistic worldview. On the demand side, the market growth is stimulated by greed and acquisitiveness. On the supply side, technocratic scientism proclaims limitless expansion and preaches a reductionistic, mechanistic philosophy, which, in spite of its success as a research program in some areas, has serious shortcomings as a worldview. As a research program, it furthers power and control, but as a worldview it leaves no room for purpose, much less for any distinction between good and bad purposes. "Anything goes" is a convenient moral stance for a growth economy because it implies that anything also sells. Expanding power and shrinking purposes lead to uncontrolled growth for its own sake. To the extent that growth has a well-defined purpose, it is limited by the satisfaction of that purpose. For example, if growth were really for the sake of the poor, we would limit it to producing things needed by the poor and would stop when the poor were no longer poor. But if growth must never stop, then we must never define our purposes too clearly, lest they should be attained and we lose our reason to grow!

VI. THE ISSUE OF OPTIMAL SCALE

If growth must never stop, then neither should we measure the costs of growth in our national accounts, lest we discover that they become equal to the benefits at the margin and thus define an optimal scale beyond which it would be anti-economic to grow! By discovering the existence of such an optimal scale, we would threaten ourselves with a question to which we do not know the answer: namely, how can we shift from a growth economy to a steady-state economy without risking economic collapse? It is nonsensical to advocate growing beyond the optimum, but politically risky to advocate nongrowth. What to do?

The answer given by some neoclassical economists is: "Don't worry, the market will automatically keep us from growing beyond any optimal scale even if such were likely, which it is not because technical progress pushes aside all apparent limits to growth."

For all its virtues, technological advance cannot escape the entropy law, nor can the market register the cost of increasing its own scale relative to the ecosystem. The market measures the relative scarcity of individual resources; it cannot measure the absolute scarcity of resources-in-general, of environmental low entropy. The best we can hope for from a perfect market is a Pareto-optimal allocation of resources.[8] Such an allocation theoretically could be attained at any scale, just as it is theoretically attainable for any distribution of income.

Most of the consequences of increasing scale are experienced as pervasive external costs. Services and amenities that were free at a smaller scale become scarce at the larger scale. We then price these newly scarce resources either by establishing new property rights or by shadow pricing. Once the growing scale has turned formerly free goods into scarce goods, then it is certainly better to give them positive prices than to continue to behave as if their price were zero. But there remains a prior question. How do we know that we were not still better off at the smaller scale, before the free good became an economic good? Perhaps we are always just making the best of an increasingly bad situation. The optimal allocation of resources (Pareto optimum) is one thing. *The optimal scale of the economy relative to the ecosystem is something else entirely.* As growth in scale forces us to turn previously free goods into economic goods, it swells GNP, but may reduce welfare, even if the newly scarce goods are optimally priced.

There is an instructive parallel between the relation of scale to the price system, and the more familiar relation of distribution to the price system. It is well known in economic theory that the price system in pure competition would attain an efficient allocation of resources in the sense of a Pareto optimum. It is further known that Pareto optimality is independent of the distribution of ownership of physical resources—that is, there is a Pareto-efficient allocation for any distribution, including unjust distributions. Therefore, the social goal of distributive justice must be pursued independently of (but not necessarily in conflict with) the price mechanism. Likewise, I suggest, for the question of scale of throughput. At any stage of growth, at any scale of throughput, the price system can optimally allocate the given volume of throughput among alternative uses. But just as nothing in the price system identifies the best distribution of ownership according to criteria of justice, neither does anything allow the price system to determine the best scale of throughput according to ecological criteria of sustainability. Just as a Pareto-optimal allocation may coexist with a socially unjust distribution, so may it coexist with an ecologically unsustainable scale. Indeed, there is a sense in which the unsustainable scale is simply an unjust distribution with respect to future generations.

Perhaps an analogy will clarify this important point. Consider a boat. Suppose we want to maximize the load the boat carries. If we place all the weight in one corner of the boat it will quickly sink or capsize. Therefore, we distribute the weight evenly. To do this, we may invent a pricing system. The heavier the load in one part of the boat the higher the price of adding another pound in that place. We allocate the weight so as to equalize the cost per additional capacity used in all parts of the boat. This is the internal equi-marginal rule for allocating space (resources) among heavy objects (alternative uses) to maximize the load carried. This pricing rule is an allocative mechanism only, a useful but dumb computer algorithm which sees no reason not to keep on adding weight and allocating it optimally until the optimally loaded boat sinks—optimally, of course—to the bottom of the sea. What is lacking is an absolute limit on scale, a recognition that the boat can displace only so much water, a rule that says: "Stop when total weight is one ton, or when the waterline reaches the Plimsoll mark." Price is only a tool for finding the optimal allocation. The optimal scale is something else. The market by itself has no criterion by which to limit its scale *vis-à-vis* its environment. Its basic thrust of exchange-value accumulation at the micro level, amplified by Keynesian policies at the macro level, is toward continuous growth in GNP which, under present conventions of national accounting, implies a growing scale of throughput.

VII. TRANSITION FROM A GROWTH TO THE STEADY-STATE ECONOMY

A realistic discussion of a transition cannot assume a blank slate, but must start with the historically given initial conditions currently prevailing. These given initial conditions I take to be the institutions of private property and the price system. These basic institutions must be bent and stretched, but not abolished, because we lack the wisdom, the leadership, and the time to replace them with something novel. This consideration lends a fundamental conservatism to a line of thought which will, nevertheless, appear quite radical to many.

A complementary design principle for guiding our speculations on the transition is to seek to combine micro freedom and variability with macro stability and control. This means, in practice, relying on market allocation of an aggregate resource throughput whose total is not set by the market, but rather fixed collectively on the basis of ecological criteria of sustainability and ethical criteria of stewardship. This approach aims to avoid both the Scylla of centralized planning and the Charybdis of the tragedy of the commons.

From its definition in the first section, it is clear that an SSE requires two kinds of limits: limits on the population of human bodies and limits on the population of artifacts. A third limit, not derivable from the definition, but important in the interest of justice, is a limit imposed on the degree of inequality in the distribution of artifacts among people—that is, limited inequality in the distribution of income. How could these three limits be institutionalized so as to achieve necessary macro-level control with the minimum sacrifice of freedom at the micro level?

The population of artifacts could be limited by controlling its "food supply," the throughput. By limiting the aggregate throughput at the point of origin (depletion), we indirectly limit the scale of physical stocks, and indirectly limit pollution outflow as well, at least in a gross quantitative sense. There remains the important problem of controlling the qualitative nature of wastes (degrees of toxicity and biodegradability), which would have to be dealt with separately by pollution taxes or standards. Several institutions could be used to limit depletion. Elsewhere I have suggested a depletion quota auction, and Talbot Page has suggested a national *ad valorem* severance tax.[9]

In the depletion quota auction, the resource market would become two tiered. In the first tier, the total amount to be extracted of each resource category would be set by a government agency and auctioned off in divisible units as rights to purchase or extract the resource up to the specified amount. Purchase of the depletion quota allows entry into the second tier of the market, which would be a private competitive market. In addition to paying the market price to the extracting company, the purchaser must present the previously purchased depletion quota rights, which the firm will present to auditors at tax time. The scheme sets total quantity centrally, but it leaves the decentralized price system to determine allocation of the fixed total among alternative uses.

The severance tax alternative is similar. By taxing depletion, we lower the throughput to some socially determined level judged to be within ecosystem tolerance limits. Once again, aggregate throughput is controlled, yet the allocation at the micro level is left to the market. The advantage of the severance tax is that it is administratively simpler. Indeed, Page argues that it amounts to nothing more than reversing the algebraic sign of the existing depletion allowances. Instead of subsidizing depletion, we would tax it. The disadvantage of the tax is that the aggregate throughput is controlled only indirectly and less tightly than with a depletion quota. Quantity as well as price is free to vary, whereas, in the quota system, all adjustment is in terms of price. The ecosystem is sensitive to quantities, not prices, so the quota system is safer ecologically. Yet the tax is surely simpler administratively and more likely to gain support as a first step.

Either of these institutions will: (1) reduce the levels of depletion and pollution, and limit the scale of the aggregate stock of artifacts; (2) raise relative prices of resources, which will force greater efficiency in resource use; and (3) result in a large revenue or rent to the government in the form either of tax or auction receipts. This third consequence ties in with limits on inequality.

Higher resource prices would by themselves most likely have a regressive effect on income distribution, much like a sales tax. However, this effect can be more than offset by distributing the receipts progressively. Inequality might be limited simply by setting minimum and maximum income limits. The minimum might work along the lines of a negative income tax and be financed by the resource rents collected by the government. In this way, we would serve the goal of ecological sustainability by limiting throughput scale, serve the goal of efficiency by high resource prices, and serve the goal of equity by redistributing the resource rents resulting from the higher prices, which, in turn, result from limits on the scale of throughput.

The minimum income and negative income tax ideas have some political support, but the maximum income idea does not. Many fear that a maximum would dull incentives and reduce growth. But if growth is no longer the *summum bonum*, then incentives at the top become less important. A range of inequality would continue to exist to reward real differences in effort, risk, and conditions of work. Incentive differentials are important, and fairness in a larger sense is certainly not served by trying to equalize all incomes. But, probably, a factor-of-ten difference would be a sufficient range of functional inequality. The incentives argument for unlimited inequality is much exaggerated, especially in the United States. Auto executives in Japan reportedly make six to eight times what assembly-line workers earn, while American auto executives make about fifteen times the wage of the unionized assembly-line worker. Futhermore, U. S. workers are laid off when sales drop, while managers keep their jobs, usually with no cut in salary, whereas in Japan everyone shares the burden of bad times. It is very clear that this large inequality has not resulted in the U.S. auto industry's being more efficient than that of the Japanese! In fact, it may be that the richer the managers become, the less incentive they have to work hard and the greater the resentment and uncooperativeness of workers who know that they will be laid off at the first sign of recession.

The proper range of inequality is a subject for further research, reflection, and debate, once the principle of a limited range of inequality is accepted.

Regarding limits to population, many possibilities exist, ranging from the coercive Chinese system to complete *laissez faire*. My own favorite institution is that first suggested by Kenneth Boulding: exchangeable birth quotas issued in an aggregate amount corresponding to replacement fertility, distributed equally among individuals, but reallocated voluntarily by sale or gift. [10] This plan combines macro control with micro freedom to a very high degree. However, the idea of having reproduction rights exchanged on a market is, for many people, unacceptable, and some cannot even distinguish between selling a legal right to reproduce and selling a baby. How some people can get so upset with this proposal while accepting the current "rent-a-womb" practices and the Nobel Laureate sperm bank for single mothers is beyond me. In any case, debate on this controversial issue detracts attention from the other institutions, which do not depend on it. Therefore, for present purposes, I will invite the reader to substitute his or her own population policy. [11] I mention this one only for the sake of completeness.

These proposed institutions have the advantage of being capable of gradual application during a transition period. Initially, the depletion quotas could be set high, near current levels (or severance taxes low), and applied first only to energy, the most general resources. The distributive limits could be initially set far apart. Birth quotas could be issued in amounts not much different from actual fertility. Once the institutions were in place the limits could be tightened, like the jaws of a vise, as gradually as desired. Of course, in a democratic society they could also be loosened to the point of being totally ineffective, if the political will be lacking.

There may, of course, be better ways of stretching and bending the institutions of private property and the market system than the ones I have suggested. But I think one is obliged to suggest something specific in the same way that an auctioneer is obliged to call out an initial price to start the bidding. The auctioneer does not believe that the first price will actually be the sale price, but without a specific starting point, the trial-and-error feedback of bidding will never get started. Nor will the feedback process of critical discussion begin as long as economists think that the concept of an SSE is not worth "bidding on"—as long as they remain committed to the illusion of growthmania.

Many further problems and issues remain in the transition to an SSE, such as international trade adjustments between growing and steady-state economies, and legitimate third world needs for further growth up to a sufficient level. These are important issues which merit discussion. But in a sense it is premature to discuss further these problems of transition as long as we have not yet firmly established the case that: (1) the growth economy is unworkable, and (2) the SSE is, in broad outline, a feasible and desirable alternative.

The first order of business is to make that case as clearly and cogently as possible. However, that is not likely to be sufficient. The Keynesian revolution did not occur because Keynes's arguments were so compellingly lucid and unanswerable. It was the Great Depression that convinced people that something was wrong with an economic theory that denied the very possibility of involuntary unemployment. Likewise, it will probably take a Great Ecological Spasm to convince people that something is wrong with an economic theory that denies the very possibility of an economy exceeding its optimal scale. But even in that unhappy event, it is still necessary to have an alternative vision ready to present when crisis conditions provide a receptive public.

Crisis conditions by themselves, however, will not provide a receptive public unless there is a spiritual basis providing the moral resources for taking purposive action—which is the point with which I began this essay. The movement toward a steady-state economy will require something like the postmodern spirituality expressed by other essays in this volume.

NOTES

1. Wes Jackson, "Six Assumptions that have Shaped American Agriculture," *Annual of Earth* 5/3 (1987), 19.

2. For a brilliant analysis of the relevance of the entropy law to economics, see Nicholas Georgescu-Roegen, *The Entropy Law and the Economic Process* (Cambridge, Mass.: Harvard University Press, 1971).

3. Frederick Soddy, *Cartesian Economics* (London: 1922). For an exposition of Soddy's economics and further references, see H. E. Daly, "The Economic Thought of Frederick Soddy," *History of Political Economy* 12/4 (1980), 469–88.

4. See Robert Heilbroner and Lester Thurow, *The Economic Problem* (Englewood Cliffs, N. J.: Prentice-Hall, 1981), 127, 135.

5. Arthur Eddington, *The Nature of the Physical World* (New York: Cambridge University Press, 1953), 74.

6. H. E. Daly, "The Circular Flow of Exchange Value and the Linear Throughput of Matter-Energy: A Case of Misplaced Concreteness," *Review of Social Economy* 42/3 (December 1985), 279–97.

7. Kenneth Boulding, "The Economics of the Coming Spaceship Earth," Henry Farrett, ed., *Environmental Quality in a Growing Economy* (Baltimore, Md.: Johns Hopkins Press, 1966).

8. A *Pareto optimum* is a state in which it is not possible to make anyone better off without causing someone to be worse off.

9. See H. E. Daly, ed., *Economics, Ecology, Ethics* (San Francisco: W. H. Freeman Co., 1980), 337–44, 317–20.

10. Kenneth Boulding, *The Meaning of the Twentieth Century* (New York: Harper & Row, 1964).

11. For an attempt at persuasion, see my *Steady-State Economics* (San Francisco: W. H. Freeman Co., 1977), 56–61.

8

AGRICULTURE IN A POSTMODERN WORLD

C. Dean Freudenberger

I. THE PROBLEM OF MODERN AGRICULTURE

Forty years ago, no one within the agricultural research and educational establishment questioned the assumption-base of contemporary agriculture. When I was an agricultural student within the California State University system, we assumed that a capital and petrochemical intensive approach to agriculture was without fault. We were experiencing the heady days of high-production yields during and following World War II. The so-called Green Revolution was in its infancy, suggesting great promise. Few people expressed concern about the future welfare of the farm family and rural community. They were prospering. International agribusiness was not yet born, because most of today's food-deficit nations were then identified as colonial possessions of Western European powers. Coffee, tea, sugar cane, groundnuts, cotton, tobacco, palm oil, copra, cocoa, and rubber occupied most of the agricultural land. Human population numbers were one-half of what they are today. Tropical deforestation and desertification were phenomena observed by only a very few agronomists and social prophets.

Agriculture was assumed to be healthy. Considerable profit-taking was realized within that colonial world. It was only in the war-torn world that questions about the importance and future of agriculture were beginning to be raised.

Today, the old colonial and post-war world has gone by. I observe that, in agriculture, we are already moving into a postmodern world. I observe this to be true because the modern world in which I was trained and served is in advanced stages of collapse, and in this crisis, alternative futures are being envisioned.

Technologically, economically, socially, and spiritually, modern agriculture everywhere is in disarray. The realization has grown that its technology is almost entirely dependent on heavy inputs of a nonrenewable, exhausting, and toxic resource: fossil fuel and petrochemicals. We now ponder the necessity of a postpetroleum technology. We are searching for a way out of growing toxicity in soils and food systems. Steadily, the growing insecurity from a mono-cropping emphasis is being realized. Today, nearly 85 percent of all food consumed by the human species comes from fourteen plants! We witness the alarming rate of species decline as a consequence of this truncation. There is a growing concern about the buildup of atmospheric carbon dioxide, largely from the oxidation of organic matter, which is but a normal consequence of annual cropping with moldboard plows. There is growing concern over the possible impact on the ozone shield from the oxidation of 100 million metric tons of nitrogen fertilizer used annually in the global food system. Old assumptions about the miracle of modern agriculture are being questioned.

Losses in topsoil are unprecedented. Given the fact that humanity has eroded away 50 percent of the earth's soil deposits and the contemporary magnitude of desertification will take another 30 percent by the end of this century, we are wondering how human populations numbering beyond six billion will be able to sustain themselves on between 5 percent and 4 percent of the earth's surface. Agriculture, closely related to global deforestation by making room for expanding cropping systems, is the most environmentally abusive activity perpetrated by the human species. Carl Sagan and others have equated its magnitude of impact with that of the threat of a nuclear winter.

Economically speaking, modern agriculture is bankrupt. In the United States, the farm debt, resting on the shoulders of 3 percent of its national population, equals the combined international debts of Mexico, Argentina and Brazil . . . about $220 billion. Gross farm income for 1988 is expected to be between $26 and $30 billion dollars. Almost every nation has organized its agriculture in anticipation of favorable international commodity markets. For many good as well as tragic reasons, that market no longer exists. Forty years of technological emphasis on crop productivity, without serious consideration of the many other essential factors, has left agriculture bankrupt almost everywhere.

Socially speaking, millions of farming units and rural communities are destitute. As Lester Brown put it in *State of the World 1986*, "The leadership in the nations simply does not understand these problems." Agriculture is the most misunderstood, complex, neglected, and unwanted subject. Yet, it is foundational to everything else. Having the subject of agriculture raised in this context is a historical first! The leaders of the Center for a Postmodern World and the Center for Process Studies need to be affirmed in their wisdom to bring this subject to the attention of contemporary philosophers and physical, social, and biological scientists.

Modern agriculture is also bankrupt spiritually. Its purpose is the generation of wealth and power. Indeed, food is now understood as a political and economic weapon. Good agriculture is defined in terms of maximized yields and wealth that can be derived from yields. Its coherence is found in these pursuits. The social, resource, and environmental costs of productivity are no longer calculated in the formulation of the idea of *good*. The welfare of the farmer, farm family, and rural community is no longer an issue. Questions about human values, community, agriculture's contribution to the welfare and enhancement of the ecosystems within which it relates, and meaningfulness of life and labor are not raised in modern agriculture. This spiritual bankruptcy is one of the major contributing causes of the farm crisis.

II. THE CONCEPT OF A REGENERATIVE, SELF-RELIANT AGRICULTURE

Emerging from the global agricultural crisis, which I have tried to describe so very briefly, is a growing recognition that alternatives must be found. It is now realized that there are no "technological fixes" (or market substitutes) for soil and vegetative erosion and species extinction. These things are quite foundational. For years, hydrophonics have been envisioned by dreamers as substitutes. But this technology is dependent on petrochemically based resources, mainly for soluble nitrogen. The seven seas have been thought to be humanity's alternative to exhausted land resources. But, like the land itself, the sea has limits to its fragile carrying capacity and we know that sea and land are deeply interdependent. Because all the frontiers of arable land have been occupied, the hope for adequate food production no longer rests on limitless prairie and forest lands. Further invasion into equatorial Africa, Latin America, and the archipelagos of Southeast Asia spells biospheric suicide. For the first time in 7,000 years of history—using the time frame of W. C. Lowdermilk in his famous writing, *The Conquest of the Land Through Seven Thousand Years*—humanity is beginning to recognize that it has not yet invented an agriculture that preserves its essential resource-base. Out of our present agricultural crisis, so firmly rooted in a long and irrevocably destructive tradition, the challenging idea of the creation of a regenerative, self-reliant agriculture is being born.

For purposes of definition and discussion, one can suggest that a regenerative agriculture involves a process of finding ways in which biological mechanisms of reproduction can be managed on a sustainable basis for the benefit of society and the future. Regenerative agriculture produces in a way that enhances the physical and biological environment, while at the same time it brings greater dignity and welfare to the producing community. A regenerative agriculture restores the "land" to a semblance of its original form. It mimics the complexity and diversity of a given natural ecosystem. It becomes an analogue of the more original biotic community. Regenerative, self-reliant agriculture visualizes the total components of an immediate environment or recognizable habitat or self-contained ecosystem, which is composed, on the one hand, of the inorganic and organic realms and, on the other, of the various organisms which live together in community, comprising the biota.

Self-reliance suggests sufficiency within a given biogeographical province (using the term suggested by the International Union for the Conservation of Nature and Natural Resources). In our moment of history, self-reliance refers to the goal of national self-sufficiency in essential food and fiber. The concept points beyond existing colonial legacies of export cropping and international trade advantages, because it gives preferred focus to the substitution of food and fiber for domestic consumption to rubber, tea, coffee, and cocoa for export. The implications are massive, and I will discuss them in a later section.

III. FOUNDATIONAL PRINCIPLES

There are three requirements for the survival of any organism, be it a salamander or a human being. They are simple to remember but awesomely challenging to practice in our modern and hoped-for postmodern world.

For an agricultural system to be considered postmodern, it must function within three principles:

1. Renewable resources are used within the productive range of the carrying capacity of the given biota.
2. All essential nonrenewables are recycled.
3. Wastes produced in the life cycle are within the limits of the absorption capacity of the biota.

These three biological and physical realities are simple to remember. To develop a food system capable of supporting the human population within these essential constraints, however, is a very different matter. This is where the challenges, as well as normative guidelines, are to be found. The biologists have pointed to these facts for many years. But the modern agricultural world has yet to take heed. The magnitude of the crisis that is now upon agriculture is beginning, however, to cause agricultural practitioners to give this set of principles a serious look.

This set of principles is the warp and woof of the tapestry of regenerative agriculture. An additional principle forms the design and holds it all together: Because all ecosystems are complex, agriculture must be coherent and consistent with this complexity. Agriculture must attempt *to optimize the biological diversity* of a given biotic community. This is the exact opposite of global monocultural cropping practices.

A postmodern agriculture therefore must, in its science, technology, and social organization, identify regenerative principles of intervention into the natural system. If this complex approach is simplified, a postmodern agriculture will not be forthcoming. The task is to achieve, at least, a symbiosis. At best, the task is to attain a high degree of complementarity of the agricultural system with the natural system. Methodologies for moving toward these principles are in their infancy . . . but at least they have been born. In this, high expectation for the actualization of a postmodern agriculture is found.

Agricultural research, educational, and extension establishments must ask: (1) What did the original ecosystem look like before extensive human intervention? (2) How did humanity relate to those earlier environments? (3) What are the relations like today? (4) What caused the transformation? (5) What can be considered an analogue of those earlier communities? (6) What are our strategies for moving from where we are to these postmodern approximations?

IV. IMPLICATIONS

By now it is obvious that envisioning a postmodern agriculture requires a totally new paradigm. It requires a radical shift from reductionism to an ecological ethos. The shift in human self-understanding which is foundational for a technological transformation requires a shift from a mechanistic paradigm to one of interrelationship.

Spiritually, postmodern agriculture points to new values, new goals, and new self-understandings as individuals and communities. It points to the values of the health of the land, of harmonious relationships in the human interface with the land, of justice between human and nonhuman life, and of meaningfulness in work and relationships. The goal of a postmodern agriculture is the enhancement of the relationships of land, agriculture and society, because a postmodern agriculture is designed to contribute to the evolutionary processes of the life of the planet on which we are so totally dependent. A postmodern agriculture is designed and engineered in ways that enhance the natural system with which it interacts. It contributes to the integrity, beauty and harmony of the natural system. Tomorrow's agriculture will reflect a spirituality of caring for the land. Caring for the land is born from the sense of gratitude for life rather than from the motivation of enlightened self-interest.

I conclude with a list of social, political, economic, and technological implications of the idea of a postmodern, regenerative and self-reliant agriculture.

1. Every nation must establish agricultural production goals that are restricted to the regenerative carrying capacity of the microbiotic communities which are found within the national political boundary. In the case of modern agricultural systems with their dependency on fossil fuel and petrochemicals, this implies up to a 50 percent reduction in agricultural production.

2. Regenerative agricultural systems require that the society pays for the costs of production of a bio-solar intensive agroeconomic system. Soil and oil and farm debt can no longer subsidize a national farm policy of abundant supplies of cheap food.

3. In a food-deficit world, international cooperation for the development of a regenerative, self-reliant food system for every nation as a replacement of the old colonial cropping systems must have first priority if biospheric survival (including human survival) is the goal.

4. Building a self-reliant and regenerative food system upon a planet supporting six to seven billion (perhaps more) human beings suggests the necessity of a moratorium on the conversion of prime agricultural land to nonagricultural uses.

5. Our global centers of agricultural research, education, and extension need to be understood as centers for the study and design of "agroecology." Farmers need to be understood (and supported with essential infrastructure) as "managers of microbiotic communities." The general society must shift its understanding of security from simple economic, political, and military powers to the maintenance of the health of the biological diversity of the whole biosphere itself. In other words, the economy, science, and technology of our time must make a shift from power acquisition and maintenance to serving the land and those who relate to the natural system in direct ways that agriculture requires. Things cannot be much longer the other way around.

6. Because a postmodern agriculture will be biologically and solar intensive, with microbiotic communities carefully rehabilitated and enhanced, coherency must exist between diversity of the microbiotic communities and numbers of people who relate to them for the purpose of maintaining domestic self-reliance in food and fiber on a regenerative basis. The necessity for nurturing the biota regeneratively dictates the numbers of biotic-community managers (farmers) needed within the society.

7. Nurturing symbiotic or complementary relationships with the natural systems requires nurturing rural community. Rural community must experience a renaissance. A regenerative agriculture cannot exist without

regenerative human communities of memory, knowledge, vision, and a sense of purpose. It is all interdependent.

8. A postmodern agriculture implies a shift in value foundations: from understanding agriculture as a way of generating wealth as its primary objective to the values of responsible freedom for responsible society, meaningfulness in life and work, the sanctity of all life, and the sanctity of the welfare of the future generations of life and their patterns of sustenance.

V. BEGINNINGS

In this nation, the work of Wes Jackson of the Land Institute at Salina, Kansas, is an illustration of a profound beginning toward a postmodern agriculture. As a plant geneticist, his approach is in enhancing certain perennial grasses in a polycultural setting. The vision is seeing the end of wheat, oats, and barley on the great prairie lands of America and establishing an analogue of the more original grassland communities.

David Hopcraft, of the 9,000-acre Game Ranching Research Center at the Athi River outside of Nairobi, has given new direction to lifestocking on semiarid rangelands. His work is cited in the Worldwatch Institute's report, *State of the World 1986*. As a third generation British background Kenyan and graduate of Cornell University in animal science, he has broken into new frontiers of vision about what he calls *natural systems management*. He has done more in building analogues of original biotic communities than any other person I have thus far encountered in my journey. The productivity of these plant and animal communities, with resource-environmental *enhancement*, is astonishing.

Many new institutions have emerged during the past fifteen years researching in the area of "integrated agroforestry." The task is, again, to rehabilitate stressed landscapes with indigenous plants (usually trees and shrubs) and to establish a new agriculture upon the knowledge and genetic stock of the predominant plant and animal communities of the recent past.

When we can get to the point of integrating perennial grasses with indigenous animal communities and, in the higher rainfall areas, integrating inland fisheries with tree crops and building our agricultural science around these foci within the various biogeographical provinces of our nation-states, then we will be seeing more clearly a postmodern agriculture. Bits and pieces of it already exist. In several Asian and Western European nations, social, economic, and political structures have already been put in place to enable a new agriculture to be born.

As mentioned at the beginning, I observe that in agriculture we are already moving into a postmodern world. I observe this to be true because the modern agricultural world in which I was trained and served for more than half a lifetime is in advanced stages of collapse. It is within the stimuli in this crisis that alternative futures are being envisioned. Significant initiatives already have been taken, both informally in the so-called organic farming movement and in private and public centers of research and development in regenerative agricultural futures. New concerns have been identified. New values are being formulated. Within the context of the global agricultural crisis, a new recognition exists that radically new alternatives have to be tried. I do not believe that many more attempts will be made to look for needed adjustments to the modern agricultural system. In many places, opportunities for a positive outcome to the crisis are being exploited. In all of this relatively new activity of the past ten to fifteen years, one begins to see the possibility and promise of a postmodern agriculture for a postmodern world.

With these new agricultural activities, one can observe a postmodern spirituality in its early stage of development. There is a central concern for earth caring—for engineering agricultural science and technology to enhance human relationships with the natural systems with which we must relate, like all life forms, for our survival. In beauty, a postmodern agriculture improves the health of the land (soil fertility and species maintenance) from generation to generation. In a postmodern agriculture, old values of wealth-accumulation and power to control and manipulate the natural system give way to cooperation and nurture as expressions of human spirituality of caring in gratitude.

SUGGESTED READINGS

Books

Lester Brown *et al., State of the World 1986* (see also *1984* and *1985*) (New York: W. W. Norton, 1986).

Lawrence Busch and William B. Lacy, *Science, Agriculture and the Politics of Research* (Boulder, Col.: Westview Press, 1983). Focuses on paralysis in U. S. agricultural research.

Don A. Dillman and Daryl J. Hobbs, *Rural Society in the U. S.: Issues for the 1980s* (Boulder, Col.: Westview Press, 1982). Focuses on social issues.

Gordon K. Douglass, ed., *Agricultural Sustainability in a Changing World Order* (Boulder, Col.: Westview Press, 1984). Selected essays by Ranil Senanayake, Stephen Gliessman, and Frederick H. Buttel.

Walter Ebeling, *The Fruited Plain: The Story of American Agriculture* (Berkeley: University of California Press, 1980).

C. Dean Freudenberger, *Food for Tomorrow?* (Minneapolis: Augsburg, 1984).

———, "Value and Ethical Dimensions of Alternative Agricultural Approaches: In Quest of a Regenerative and Just Agriculture," Kenneth A. Dahlberg, ed., *New Dimensions for Agriculture and Agricultural Research: Neglected Dimensions and Emerging Alternatives* (Totowa, N. J.: Rowman & Allenheld, 1986).

J. Donald Hughes, *Ecology in Ancient Civilizations* (Albuquerque: University of New Mexico Press, 1975).

Wes Jackson, Wendell Berry, and Bruce Colman, eds. *Meeting the Expectations of the Land: Essays in Sustainable Agriculture and Stewardship* (San Francisco: North Point, 1984).

W. C. Lowdermilk, *Conquest of the Land Through Seven Thousand Years,* Agriculture Information Bulletin No. 99 (Washington, D. C.: U. S. Department of Agriculture, Soil Conservation Service, Government Printing Office, 1978).

David and Marcia Pimentel, *Food, Energy and Society* (New York: Halsted Press [John Wiley and Sons], 1979).

R. Neil Sampson, *Farmland or Wasteland: A Time to Choose* (Emmaus, Penn.: Rodale, 1981). Focuses on environmental and agricultural resource crises.

Journals

Agriculture and Human Values, ed. Richard Haynes. Department of Philosophy, University of Florida, Gainesville, Florida 32611.

Alternative Agriculture News, ed. Garth Youngberg. Institute for Alternative Agriculture, Inc., 9200 Edmonston Road, Suite 117, Greenbelt, Maryland 20770.

9

TOWARD A POSTMODERN SCIENCE AND TECHNOLOGY

Frederick Ferré

I use the word *technology* to refer to all practical implementations of intelligence. Technology, understood broadly in this way, played its vastly important role on our planet long before the recent appearance of what we call science. Technology, not science, *directly* touches lives and impinges on nature. It is a primary phenomenon of human culture. No culture lacks its characteristic technologies.

European technologies, of course, were radically transformed, primarily during the past two centuries, by the influence of modern science; and such new technologies have in turn transformed large portions of our world into what is sometimes, by extension, called *modern scientific civilization*. Today, however, as evidenced by the first volume in this series, we see the exciting possibility of an emerging postmodern science, [1] reordered in ways that could make it—and the artifacts and attitudes associated with it—as different from typical modern science and civilization as *they* were, in their turn, distinct from premodern ways of thought and practice.

Practice, of course, involves values. Technology is obviously the embodiment of far more than thought alone. It is no less fundamentally the

133

incarnation of needs and values. We express our hopes, fears, desires, revulsions, and preferences through the implements we make and use—or forbid. Technology has always been the nodal point where facts and values, knowledge and purpose, effectively come together. Both aspects count as necessary conditions: lacking *knowledge*, on the one hand, we could not shape tools to our ends, no matter how intensely we might affirm them; but lacking *values*, on the other hand, we would never be motivated to set our knowledge to work. The *valued* and the *known* are essential ingredients in every artifact. Unpack them and we find a whole world of commitments and beliefs.

I. FROM PREMODERN TO MODERN TECHNO-WORLDS

It would be overly simple to lump together all the worlds of commitment and belief before the rise of modern science as though there were only one premodern world. Doing so would gloss over the vast differences, for example, between the gentle and decentralized premodern Hopi Indian culture and the premodern "mega-machine," as Lewis Mumford called it,[2] of Pharaonic Egypt. It would blur the contrasts between premodern technologies of the bullock and hoe, on the one hand, and equally premodern technologies of the horse and sword, on the other.

Still, there is no doubt that something even more radical differentiates our world of modern technologies from all such other techno-worlds which predate us or still manage to coexist on the planet with us. What does *premodern* mean, then, not described merely as "earlier" than our modern culture, but analyzed by its key characteristics?

First, a crucial trait of all the many premodern technological worlds is found in the way that premodern artifacts and techniques tend to be created and disseminated. The key to premodern technology is "practical reason." Practical reason is the capacity to devise, recognize, and repeat effective methods of accomplishing mentally envisioned ends. Whether those ends may involve peacefully creating a pottery bowl or smithing a bronze sword, whether they involve organizing farmers for a village planting or controlling platoons of slaves to build a pyramid, is not the main point. What links them all at a level below even such important differences is their reliance on *methods derived by trial and error,* perpetuated by *tradition and rule of thumb.* The wisdom of the farmer, the lore of metalsmith, the secrets of the herbalist, the techniques of the guild—these are passed on from master to apprentice, mother to daughter, priest to acolyte. Such methods are precious because they capture and perpetuate the happy coincidences of past discovery.

Second, premodern technology, like grandmother's best recipe, is generally *inexact*. Add a "pinch" of this, bake in a "moderately" hot oven, knead until it "feels right"—practical reason is content with approximations, as it must be without precision instruments. But, over the long run provided by stable tradition, approximations sometimes average out and eliminate random errors. Babylonian priest observers, for example, made remarkably reliable calendars, including even the prediction of lunar eclipses, on the basis of hundreds of years of imprecise astronomical approximations. Medieval master builders, without exact engineering knowledge or modern materials, erected breathtaking cathedrals to the glory of God. The accumulation of practical lore represented by the agricultural revolution eventually freed Europe to create the modern world.

Third, despite all such impressive achievements, premodern technology is based only on the practical knowledge *that* something works, not *why* it works. *Theory*, in other words, *follows rather than leads practical success*. Because we are thinking creatures, theories do arise purporting to explain. The Babylonians, for example, invented elaborate theological accounts of motives for the sometimes apparently irregular behavior of the "divine" planets to explain to themselves their successes as calendarmakers. Some cultures, like the ancient Canaanites, explained the success of their agricultural techniques by theories of sympathetic sexual magic, and consequently linked their springtime farm labors, penetrating the earth by seed, to orgies of intercourse in the fields by night. We smile today at such notions, and although we might grant the Canaanites their uninhibited exertions, our mechanized crops yield many times more from artificial fertilizers than those ancient farmers, heated in ritual copulation, ever could have dreamt of. What happened? What is the secret of modern technology and the modern world?

The secret is no secret. We all know that it was the rise of what we loosely call *science* that changed our world by transforming all technologies, both benign and malignant. The change was literally radical. It entered from the intellectual root by grafting theoretical to practical reason, for the first time in human history. That is, the crucial new factor is *thought* engaged in exact theory, disciplined by logic and empirical verification.

Modern science, we must note, is itself a hybrid of thought and practice. Modern science could never have arisen without such highly developed premodern craft techniques as European glassmaking (to produce Galileo's lenses and Toricelli's barometer), which provided practical implementation for answering theoretical questions. Thus, both modern science and modern technology are blends of theoretical and practical reason. They mutually made each other possible.

What key differences were made by grafting theoretical to practical reason—differences so striking that we date the new, "modern" era from this point? The first great difference that this made to reshaping the world was that *verifiable theory began to lead technological practice*. It became *practical* to learn theory; to investigate the "inner springs and levers" of the natural order; to discover how to "obey nature in order to rule her."

The second great difference was that *theoretical ideals of precision* replaced the "close enough" expectations of the practical arts. Valves were ground to finer and finer tolerances to approximate the impossible ideal of the perfectly efficient heat machine imagined by the physics of Carnot. Such ideals spread widely. Farmers, turned agribusinessmen, could no longer tolerantly shrug off losses to bird and insect "pests," but struggled toward the impossible ideal of the 100 percent return on invested labor, energy, and material.

The third epoch-making difference, finally, was the invention, as Whitehead put it, of the *method of invention*. Technologies no longer needed to arise by some happy stroke at moments of crisis or need, to be perpetuated by tradition. Modern technologies are developed—and potential "needs" (or at least potential markets) are envisioned—by theoretical inferences about what should work, what might be possible to do or make. Einstein's letter to President Franklin Roosevelt, outlining the possibility of a bomb based on a new source of energy, shown theoretically possible by abstract mathematics and supported by a few highly inferential experiments, is only one example—although a chillingly apt one—of modern theoretical reason leading the way to its practical implementation. The resulting Manhattan Project, the building and repeated use of the atomic bomb, the endless arms race, the policies of Mutually Assured Destruction, the nuclear power industry, and now the burgeoning of "star wars" projects around the techno-scientific world are all examples of modern knowledge and values blended and embodied.

II. FROM MODERN TO
POSTMODERN TECHNO-WORLDS

It would be unfair and too simple to suggest that such examples are the only ones in which modern knowledge and values are incarnated. Like premodern technologies, modern technologies also show vital contrasts in the moral qualities of the ends sought. Radio and television were suggested by Hertz's theory before the technology was implemented by which music and messages now fill our ears; theories in genetics now suggest possibilities for agricultural technologies that may someday give corn the capacity to manufacture its own insecticides or, still further in the future, to fix its own nitrogen from the soil.

The prime fact remains, however, that the dominant methods of theorizing associated with the rise of modern science, and now incarnate everywhere in our surrounding technosphere, have a characteristic "tilt"—toward simplification and reductive analysis—that might not have been that way, except by historical circumstance, and might not forever be associated with good scientific work in the future. If the transition from premodern to modern technology was mainly characterized by theoretical intelligence being radically grafted to practical craft intelligence, then the transition from the modern to the postmodern world may require a no less radical transformation in the qualitative "tilt" of theoretical intelligence itself.

The point is not to reject theoretical intelligence as such. Short of a universal catastrophe, naturally or technologically caused—one that plunges the whole world into barbarism or worse—we shall need more than ever to continue leading our *praxis* by *theoria*. Given this actual overcrowded world as our starting point, we can ill afford nostalgic longing for clumsy and slow premodern ways. We need precision. We need a method for guiding our inventions. But theoretical intelligence needs radical overhaul.

This may not be so unthinkable as it sounds at first. Much of the methods and fundamental assumptions of modern theoretical intelligence might have been historical accident, not something built into theorizing as such. Think what a different face *theoria* might wear today, had astronomy and physics not been the lead sciences of the early modern era! Astronomy, after all, is the grand domain in which the simplifying theoretical ideals of "frictionless motion" and "eternal regularity" are nearly approximated for human observers. In some ways, the human race was profoundly fortunate that astronomy could lead the way. Would we have had any science at all if it had not been for those visible cosmic regularities that tempted us to theorize? If, by some small meteorological alteration in the earth's atmosphere, our skies at night had always been overcast, could the hurly-burly of terrestrial events ever have given us the idea that behind all the hubbub and complexity of events there might lie intelligible form? But, sadly, at the same time, the early triumph of astronomy and physics—the sciences of the simple and the dead—gave the "tilt" to the character of scientific theorizing that has fostered mechanistic, deterministic, reductionistic, alienating assumptions about the "really real"—assumptions that have come back to haunt us not only in the forging of our characteristic weapons, with their unprecedented capacity for omnicide, but also in the fashioning of our most "successful" technologies of economic exploitation, with their unsustainable rapacity against the earth.

Is there another way? Surely there is at least no logical necessity that theorizing, once begun, must remain forever locked into the mechanistic, reductionistic models of reality drawn from astronomy and classical physics. In recent decades, the new physics itself has been struggling to break free from those modern models toward something radically different. But perhaps the best example of the seeds of a fundamentally new approach to scientific thinking—one that radically accepts *complexity* as its proper domain and *synthesis* as its cognitive aim (though still demanding precision and using modern analysis as its tool)—can be found germinating in the vulnerable new science of ecology. To be itself, to do its proper job, ecology must begin and end with large, complex systems of living, interacting organisms and their inorganic settings. Its essential aim is to understand whole living systems. Between the beginning and the end, it uses the tools of rigorous analysis, not with the modern reductionist assumption that understanding the parts separately will somehow add up to the whole, but with the significantly different aim to discover more precisely how within this whole the parts are differentiated and mutually interactive, essentially influenced by the complex relationships in which they interact and in turn essentially influencing the whole.

Caution is in order. This vision of an emerging postmodern science may be a mirage. Ecology is, in fact, an embattled ground today, with analyzers and reducers competing for leadership with the pioneering synthesizers. The grip of reductionist ideals is immensely strong within all the sciences, including ecology, and most sources of funding are in the hands of those who tend to define scientific "success" by traditional results rather than by a more gradual, unfolding understanding of complex wholes. Still, this vision of an alternative approach to "doing" science—systematic, synthesizing, and radically inclusive, even of the investigator—not only continues to inspire many ecologists but also seems required in other sciences ranging from quantum mechanics to cybernetics. What types of technologies, what sort of civilization, might incarnate such postmodern sciences and values?

One urgent need for our world, looked at from the "whole downward" instead of from the "parts upward," is for effective and humane controls on human population. Postmodern birth control technologies must allow the world, particularly in those areas now groaning under poverty and overpopulation, to break destructive cycles so that standards of life can rise above the tide of hungry mouths. It is natural for us to think first of bioengineered solutions. A simple and reversible birth control method for males, perhaps by pill or injection, will not long remain beyond reach. But a far more genuinely postmodern approach would be to accept such technical wonders of bioengineering as sophisticated tools within the effective context of higher-order, carefully designed societal methodologies aimed at optimizing well-being for the whole of humankind. Rather than "engineering" fertility by manipulating small parts of the whole, the aim would be to implement a planetwide network of supporting social relations. This implies, for example, the practical implementation of worldwide systems to provide old-age security, thereby obviating the perceived need for large families; the implementation of systems to provide universal education, particularly emphasizing the education of young women, thus simultaneously generating wider ranges of responsible choice and delaying the starting point of reproduction; the implementation of systems to distribute populations and resources more equitably around the globe; and the implementation of other theory-led, precise and critically examined systems of benign postmodern socio-technology that could sustain the health and equilibrium of an interdependent human population on a finite Earth.

Bioengineering, under the balance-seeking influence of ecological thinking, could make profoundly significant changes possible in the technology of food production. Our modern tendencies have been to force bioengineering into the service of maximized yields, but if "optimization" replaces "maximization" as the postmodern ideal, and if social contexts of well-being are considered, a different set of possibilities would arise. Corn, genetically engineered to fix its own nitrogen and to produce its own pesticides, for example, could be raised in many more locations, thereby requiring less centralized production methods than in modern agribusiness. There would be a trade-off, no doubt, in yield per stalk, because the law of conservation of energy applies to biology no less than physics, and the additional energy required by the plant for taking on such new functions would need to be diverted from somewhere, almost certainly from yield. But if optimization for the good of the whole is truly the aim, then low-till, decentralized food production could be paid for by deliberately relinquishing the aim of maintaining the largest possible head on the smallest possible stalk.

More diversity in genetic types, modified for different regions and conditions, even tastes, would be allowed by such a postmodern agricultural technology. This would lead to a healthier biosphere, less prone to cataclysmic losses from unanticipated blights or pests. True, it might be more expensive per plant unit, and almost certainly less efficient of calories per stalk; but the added diversity of agricultural sites, including suburban and even urban plots, could balance these losses. What could probably not be sustained, on this scenario, would be the vast current production of grains for feeding to animals destined for our tables. But perhaps the postmodern world will be a world voluntarily much more abstemious of meat-eating than is our modern Big Mac society. Ethical issues concerning respect due to animals, and to the natural environment, are on the leading edge of ethical sensibility today. The larger context to be considered must not be limited to the human race alone. Perhaps the postmodern world will not be wholly vegetarian—that would be a break with the symbolic as well as the real ecological cycles within which human life is lived—but surely, flesh-eating might be expected to become a rarer sacrament.

Patterns of human reproduction, the shape of agriculture—these are fundamental to any society, but they are only two examples from a vast array of ways in which technologies incarnating postmodern ways of knowing and valuing could create a new world for future living. The list of important examples is endless. How will habits of systematic thought within postmodern science influence our housing? Will the ideal of the private dwelling, isolated from the rest of the community and radiating energy from all four walls, gradually give way to dwelling technologies in which privacy enough to allow healthy differentiation will be possible within a more socially interactive and ecologically sound framework? Again, how will ideals of ecological balance and systematic integrity influence our transportation technologies? Will some combination of the freedoms of private transportation with the social integration and ecological responsibility of public systems be achievable? What about police technologies in the postmodern world? Technologies of entertainment? What of the relations between the technologies and the religions of the world in the future?

III. PARADOXES OF POSTMODERNITY

To clarify the nature of our present situation, poised as we are between the modern world and the possibility of a postmodern world, let us consider some paradoxes of postmodernity. First paradox: *Our key word,* postmodern, *itself contains a tension.* On one meaning, it merely points away from the present, "after-the-now," and *could have any content*; but *we are hoping to give it a content*, a set of moral and epistemological characteristics, as though we knew what the world after-the-now is going to be like. We do not. Just as there were many premodern worlds of practice and belief incarnate in various technologies, and just as there are now qualitatively different technologies within the modern world, we must anticipate a variety of possible postmodern worlds. The practices of putting theoretical priority on synthesis, the scientific subordination of reduction to integration, the replacement of the technological ideal of maximization with that of optimization, are like tender shoots growing among the massive concrete blocks of reductionist science and its resulting tunnel-vision technology. We must remember that we are speaking from hope, not from knowledge, when we name the future after organic forces that are sometimes scarcely visible in our time. The first paradox of postmodernity is that it *refers without referring to anything actual.* It is a comparative expression still with only one actual term in the comparison. It expresses our dissatisfaction with aspects of the present; but *it must not lull us into supposing that the future is already laid out as we would wish it to be.*

Second paradox: What we view now as the tender shoots of the postmodern may *look different from but at the same time much like the modern.* Although in Galileo's time many of the issues, much of the jargon. and all the disputes were set in ways that seemed (and were) continuous with the thinking and practices of premodernity, Galileo's fundamental starting points—in mathematical formulation and empirical confirmation—eventually changed the world. In the same way, at present, everything may look continuous. All the modern sciences pay reverence in principle to synthesis, after all. Sometimes, indeed, they pay more than lip service! The Newtonian synthesis, modeling the universe as a vast mechanical system, was the paradigmatic triumph of modern thinking, was it not? In our day, ecologists use chemical and other forms of analysis to understand what is going on in their complex ecosystems. Where, then, is the historic difference? The paradox arises because from apparently small differences of emphasis, starting point, and goal, great differences can flow. The mere presence of system or synthesis is not enough; its quality matters, too. Consider the difference between a mechanical and an organic system. The parts of a mechanical system, such as a watch, continue to be just what they are removed from the system; the parts of an organism, torn from their context, do not. The watch is dead; its value is always extrinsic; its function is supplied from outside itself. The organism is alive; it has intrinsic value for itself; its functions are internally directed for the sake of the living entity as a whole. Likewise, consider the difference between beginning an inquiry with the conviction that looking into the microstructure of the parts is primary to reconstructing a theory of the whole, on the one hand, and beginning with the conviction that only an initial appreciation of the properties of the whole can guide effective research into the parts, on the other. These seemingly small differences in attitude and starting place, once incarnated in technological artifacts and social practice, can make all the difference to the world of postmodernity.

Finally, third paradox: Bringing about the postmodern world we prefer *is not up to us but, at the same time, it is up to us*. The forces are too large and the time frames too long for any of us to bring a world about by our own efforts. Heidegger is right, on one level, to warn against manipulative activism, as though we could engineer history to our tastes. Such attitudes, in any case, would betray in us the continued dominance of a typically mechanistic control-syndrome. There are contexts—and this is one—in which we must acknowledge the appropriateness of language about "destiny." Still, it will only be by persons engaged with ideas and values at the nodal junctions of historical change that the postmodern world—of whatever character—will be realized. Our ability to recognize our "historical moment" is not wholly up to us any more than the character of the moment itself is of our voluntary making. But *there is a freedom in human agents to turn toward or to turn away from the quiet lure of better real possibilities*. In the multitude of these turnings, both in our minds and in our material implements, the postmodern world will, for worse or for better, gradually be determined.

NOTES

1. See also my *Shaping the Future: Resources for the Post-Modern World* (New York: Harper & Row, 1976).

2. Lewis Mumford, *The Myth of the Machine,* Vol. 1: *Technics and the Human Development* (New York: Harcourt, Brace & World, 1967); Vol. 2: *The Pentagon of Power* (1970).

10

PEACE AND THE POSTMODERN PARADIGM

David Ray Griffin

A *paradigm* is both a worldview and an ethic—a way of ordering our lives—implied by this worldview. In this essay, I focus on the question of how the *modern* paradigm, which has increasingly dominated our culture since the seventeenth century, has contributed to various crises making world peace so difficult today, and how a *postmodern* paradigm would help alleviate these crises and make peace more realizable.

A basic failure of modern thought has been to underestimate the extent to which we are *religious* beings. By this I mean that we seek *meaning* (however unconsciously), and that we do this by trying to be *in harmony with the ultimate nature of the world*, as we perceive it. Modern thought has suggested that religion was a mere transitory state, something we are now outgrowing. Modernity hence ignored the degree to which the *modern cosmology* would create a *new kind of human being*, a new way of being human. Modernity has tried to pretend that we could go on being essentially the same kind of people, with most of the same kinds of values and relationships, even though we have come to adopt a view of the world and ourselves that differs essentially from all those views that have stood the test of time. Modernity has even come up with a derogatory name—"the naturalistic fallacy"—for the idea that our ethic should be based upon our cosmology, that how we *ought* to live should be based upon our view of the *nature* of things. [1] Having dubbed this a fallacy, moderns could cheerfully continue propogating the fragmented, disenchanted, power-based, competitive worldview of modernity, releasing themselves from all responsibility for the behavior of the people to whom this new way of seeing reality is spread.

A basic aspect of a postmodern consciousness is the recovery of the fact that our cosmology, our worldview, inevitably determines our ethic, our way of living. As Carl Becker put it: "The desire to correspond with the general harmony springs perennial in the human breast." [2] From a postmodern point of view, accordingly, the question of truth and the question of action cannot be separated. [3] We will not overcome the present disastrous ways of ordering our individual and communal lives until we reject the view of the world upon which they were based. And we cannot reject this old view until we have a new view that seems more convincing. The modern paradigm will die only as a postmodern paradigm begins to emerge.

Part of the motivation for examining postmodern options comes from fully realizing how destructive the modern worldview and its attendant ethic have been. In this essay, I focus on four aspects of the modern worldview that have helped make world peace so difficult today, suggesting the way a postmodern paradigm would lead to a better way of living together on our planet.

I. THE NATURE OF POWER

One destructive feature of the modern paradigm was that it made *coercive power the basis of all change.* In the first stage of modernity, which was theistic, the omnipotent God was the source of all motion. The fashioners of the modern view of God—Descartes, Boyle, Newton, and their voluntaristic forerunners—stressed the omnipotence of God even more than had the major medieval theologians. They made the power of God more important than the divine love, and they portrayed this power as manipulating the world from outside. God became a purely external creator, creating and controlling the world through sheer force. The message of this theology was that it is brute power—whether motivated by love or not—that "makes the world go 'round." Because our basic religious motive is to be in harmony with what is ultimately real and effective, religious motivation led moderns to make coercive power basic to their relations—those with other families, other companies, other countries, other religions.

Besides giving us a bad model to imitate, the omnipotent God of first-stage modern thought led to intolerant attitudes. Belief in an omnipotent God—in the sense of one who acts unilaterally in the world, not being dependent upon our response—leads naturally to belief in an infallible revelation. This infallible revelation is taken as announcing the One True Way, making all the other ways by definition false, even blasphemous. The desire to imitate deity by coercing others was accordingly reinforced by the conviction that in destroying one's *own* enemies one was destroying *God's* enemies. In this implicit and only semilogical reasoning, of course, one forgot to ask how, if God is determining all things, there could be some people who do not believe the right things!

In second-stage modern thought, there is no God. Many second-stage moderns have assumed that atheism would promote better human relations: there would be no omnipotent God to imitate, no vengeful, arbitrary divine will to obey, no infallible revelation of the One True Way. The atheistic humanists wold be gentle, modest, empirical, and solve their differences by rational suasion. This conclusion assumed the superficial view of second-stage modernity, which holds that religious attitudes and behavior point to nothing permanent and will fade away with the death of God. But second-stage modern thought has generated its own kind of religious values and behavior.

With regard to many issues, it is much different from first-stage modernity, but not with regard to the questions of power and tolerance. It is still power that makes the world go 'round. Now, however, it is the power of cells, molecules, atoms, and subatomic particles, which are assumed to interact by coercive impact. The whole of the world, inorganic and organic alike, including the finest achievements of human beings, are said to be nothing but the result of the power-relationships among these basic entities. Darwinian theory is the quintessential modern theory, saying that competition, the "struggle for survival," is the basic law of life. "Social Darwinism" is the ethic only imperfectly concealed in the "purely scientific" theory of evolution.[4] It is the view that we should imitate nature in being competitive, even ruthless, letting only the "fit" survive; by selfishly seeking our own good, as "nature" does, we will actually promote the good of the whole.

Nontheistic modern thought has also been little more tolerant than the theistic form. Although it claims to reject an infallible revelation in favor of experience and reason, its own version of experience and reason, dubbed the *Scientific Method*, which has all sorts of ontological as well as methodological presuppositions built in, becomes the new One True Way.[5] The views of other cultures are automatically labeled *false, superstitious, primitive, unenlightened, unprogressive*. They are not seen as worthy of respect. The arrogance of the missionary representatives of Modern Science has been at least as great as that of the representatives of previous incarnations of the One True Way.

Postmodern thought would create new attitudes. It again speaks of God, but its God is not the God of medieval or early modern thought. For those who cannot break the connection between the word and this previous image, the word *God* should not be used, at least for a time. Perhaps *Holy*

Reality is better. The Holy Reality is our Creator, but not in an external, unilateral sense. This Holy Reality stimulates us from within, urging us to create ourselves in optimal fashion; this Holy Reality moves us by giving us a dream, not a push. To imitate this Holy One is to provide others with visions by which they can realize their own deepest potentialities for creativity.

Postmodern thought, furthermore, portrays the fundamental relationships of life as noncoercive, and shows that cooperation is more basic in the nature of things than competition. Coercive relations and competition do exist, but they are derivative, secondary. To have a postmodern consciousness is to see and feel the primacy of cooperation, mutual assistance, and noncoercive relations. An ethic informed by this consciousness will not feel violence to be a satisfactory way of achieving goals.

II. THE NATURE OF NATURE

A second feature of the modern paradigm with negative consequences for world peace has been its *materialistic view of nature.* First-stage modern thought was dualistic; second-stage modernity has been totally materialistic. But both have understood "nature" materialistically. And both have been disastrous.

The materialistic view of nature sees it as exhaustively comprised of insentient bits of matter, devoid of all experience, all feelings, all internal relations, all purposive activity, all striving—in short, all intrinsic value. Max Weber has pointed to this "disenchantment of the world" as one of the main features of the modern period. Nature is seen as dead—as composed of inert objects and as having no living presence of deity in it. This "Death of Nature"[6] has had diverse destructive consequences.

In the first stage of modernity, this materialistic view of nature was part of a dualistic-theistic worldview. Human beings, by virtue of their unique souls or minds, were said to be totally different in kind from the world of natural things. We, in Kant's phrase, were "ends in ourselves," not to be used as mere instruments for realizing someone else's ends. Each of us was to be regarded as a Thou, not merely an It, because each of us was a subject, not a mere object. But the world of nature was regarded as a world of objects. Natural things were properly regarded as mere Its, to be used for our purposes. In fact, God had created nature for the sake of human beings.

This first-stage modern worldview hence produced a radically *anthropocentric ethic:* human desires and satisfactions were the only ones that had to be considered in deciding the way to treat nature. And this meant an *exploitative ethic:* not only was there no sentience and intrinsic value in nature to be considered; God also had explicitly made the world to be dominated (read "exploited") by us. Not to exploit nature would be to fail to realize the *imago dei* in us. As Carolyn Merchant and many others have pointed out, this radically dualistic worldview, with its radically anthropocentric ethic, was used, and was in part constructed, to justify the vivisection of and experimentation on animals, the mining of the earth, and other practices discouraged by the older reverential attitudes toward nature.[7] The uninhibited program to plunder nature has increased the competition between individuals, corporations, and nations, as each seeks to possess and control as much of the world's "natural resources" as possible. This drive has been a major cause of colonization (including neocolonization), mass enslavement, and war in modern times.

This anthropocentric, exploitative ethic was a first consequence of the materialistic view of nature; a second consequence was an increased tendency to treat other human beings, especially women and "primitives," as mere objects. The view that all human beings have souls, of course, should have led to a radically egalitarian ethic, and it has in some writers. But the practice of regarding some parts of the world as mere objects, totally devoid of intrinsic value and of deity, made it easier, by force of habit, to treat other human beings as mere objects, especially women and dark-skinned peoples, which many European males regarded as "more natural," hence, less fully human. These ideas were used to justify keeping women out of business and political life. Most of the modern institutions, and their conflicts, have thereby developed without benefit of the quite different perceptions and values women would have brought had they been in positions of leadership. These ideas were also used to justify the enslavement and even decimation of "primitives," in order to allow the "fully human" Europeans to populate the planet and develop it.

Furthermore, dualism proved itself very difficult to maintain theoretically, especially after evolutionary ideas became accepted. In second-stage modernity, both God and the unique human soul fade. No God exists to command love and justice in the treatment of others, and the others have no soul which sets them apart as "ends in themselves." Other people become mere instruments for the purposes of those who have power. Here we reach what Max Weber lifts up as the distinctive attitude of modernity: *Zweckrationalität*—a purely instrumental rationality, which considers only means, not ends.

Today, the modern world oscillates in confusion between dualism and total materialism. Its theoretical position has increasingly become materialistic: dualism is considered untenable by most modern scientists and philosophers. But, in practice, moderns operate with an anthropocentric ethic—at least for themselves and those they care about. The soul is said to be unreal (an "epiphenomenon") and yet to be the one thing that has absolute value and hence absolute rights! Having no distinct soul, the human being is said to be as fully determined as everything else; yet human freedom must be protected! No consistent ethic can be based upon such confusion. And no ethic that will reverse the exploitative and war-creating tendencies of modernity will be developed until a postmodern vision of the world becomes prevalent, one in which nothing is a mere object to be exploited with impunity, in which all people and all things are seen as embodying the Holy.

Besides an exploitative ethic, first in relation to "nature" and then also in relation to other humans, another consequence of the "disenchantment of the world" has been the loss of a sense of kinship with nature, and a loss of meaning and satisfaction derived from communion with nature. (Sartre's *Nausea* gives a graphic description.) With this loss, substitutes had to be found, because humans *demand* meaning and some satisfaction in living. The meaning has increasingly been found not by living in harmony with the rhythms of nature, but by controlling and dominating it. The satisfactions have been increasingly sought through "artificial" means, through the possession of the products of technology. The disenchantment of nature has thereby resulted in a more acquisitive type of human being. Human beings for whom the very meaning of life is tied to acquisitions are more prone to want more than they need, and to resort to violence to get it.

A closely related consequence of the materialistic view of nature has been the tendency to *equate the real and the material*. Because our religious drive is to be in harmony with the real, materialism thus makes us want to be in harmony with material things and processes. We show that we are "in harmony with" matter by possessing and controlling it. The religious drive of modernity, therefore, has been manifested in the twin drives to amass wealth and to develop technological mastery over nature. "Progress" has virtually become equated with the increase in material wealth and technological mastery (so much so that it takes explicit reflection to realize that there are other notions of what constitutes true progress, for example, "growth in grace," or "spiritual maturation"). Progress in this sense, as has been documented by many writers, has become the modern religion replacing older notions of, say, the expectation of the Realm of God on earth.[8] This attitude, combined with the alienation from nature, has increased the tendency to gain control of the natural world and its resources at all costs. The same religious drive that once led people, given their understanding of the Holy, to embark on Holy Wars in the name of God or Allah, was now directed by a new understanding of the ultimate nature of things, and hence of the Holy. Many of the modern wars, and the relentlessness with which the development of technology has been pursued, simply cannot be understood apart from realizing that the modern West is no less religious than any other society. Its piety simply takes a radically different form from that of any previous society. The self-destructive path on which the world has been set, as it has been increasingly dominated by the paradigm of the modern West, can only be altered by developing a new worldview and thereby a new ethic. This will require "the reenchantment of the world."[9] A postmodern paradigm will help bring about just that.

III. THE NATURE OF HUMAN NATURE

A third feature of the modern paradigm with negative consequences for world peace has been its *one-sided view of human nature*. Modern thought has viewed human beings under various reductionistic abstractions. One modern view has been that the sexual drive is the only thing that really moves us. But the most pervasive abstraction has been *homo oeconomicus*, which treats human beings as if economic motives were all-determining. Madison Avenue seems to base most of its advertising upon the conviction that some combination of these two drives motivates all human behavior. Both of these are based upon *receptive values*, in which the person is primarily a passive recipient of enjoyment. Much of our public life reflects the assumption that receptive values are all that are necessary for a satisfactory human life. All we need is enough food, shelter, technological gadgets, and sexual stimulation. This assumption reflects the modern view of the world, according to which it is comprised of passive, inert substances. The first-stage modernists did distinguish between the activity of the human soul and the passivity of nature. But quite soon moderns started seeing themselves in the image of nature. What did remain of their "activity" became reduced mainly to the domination and possession of natural things.

The truth, according to postmodern thinking, is that we are motivated by all sorts of values. I distinguish between *receptive* values, *achievement* or *self-actualizing* values, and *contributory* values. This classification is based upon the recognition that we are essentially *creative* beings: all individuals embody creative energy, and we humans evidently embody it to the highest degree (at least on this planet). We receive the creative contributions from others; this receptivity, with many of its values (for example, food, water, air, and aesthetic and sexual enjoyment), is an essential aspect of our natures. But we also are creative. We need to actualize our potentials, to achieve something on our own. Furthermore, we need to make a contribution to others: this drive is as essential to our human being as the needs to receive and to achieve. This more adequate appreciation of the need to enjoy creative as well as receptive values has been fundamental to most feminist writers.

The failure to recognize the essential creativity of all human beings and the correlative assumption that the receptive values are alone essential leads those with political and economic power to form unrealistic policies. In establishing factories, for example, the modern assumption has been that, as long as the workers made enough money and did not have to work too hard, they would be content. A postmodern orientation would have told them what some have been discovering only recently—that the workers are not just "workers"; they are people, and as such they want to get some satisfaction from their job, to do something creative, to feel they are making a worthwhile contribution to something, and to participate in the decision-making processes of the company. Powerful nations, in relation to less powerful ones, have likewise ignored these other nations' desires to take pride in their own nation, to see it making its own decisions, and to see it as making important contributions to the world community.

World peace is endangered just as much by actions and attitudes that wound the pride of other nations and thwart their desires to exercise their creativity as it is by actions that threaten receptive values. One task of postmodern thought is to create a consciousness in which the need to experience self-actualizing and contributory values is recognized to be as essential to the life of individuals, communities and nations as is the need to feel they are getting their fair share of essential receptive values.

IV. THE NATURE OF RELATIONS

A fourth feature of the modern paradigm, which has had all sorts of negative consequences for world peace, is its *nonecological view of existence*. An ecological view is one in which individuals are seen to be *internally related* to each other; each is internally constituted by its relations to the others and its response thereto. The seventeenth-century thinkers defined the basic bits of matter comprising nature as totally independent substances, which are not internally affected by the things in their enviroment. Their relations to each other were regarded, in other words, as wholly external, as not entering into them in any constitutive way. Even the human soul was thought to be entirely context-independent by these first-stage moderns. For example, Descartes said that a human soul is a "substance" as much as is a bit of matter, and a "substance" he defined as "that which requires nothing but itself to be what it is." A less ecological start for the modern world could not be imagined!

These first-stage moderns were simply creating nature in the image of their God, who was the nonecological being *par excellence*. In conceiving God as totally omnipotent, immutable, and impassible, of course, they were simply carrying on the tradition of classical theism, which had long since relinquished the Bible's view of a God who genuinely interacts with the creation. The nonecological view of human beings, and of creatures in general, with which the modern world began is another example of the power of the religious motive. In this case, we defined ourselves into harmony with the nonrelational God of premodern thought by conceiving ourselves to be just as nonrelational as He was. (The masculine pronoun is used advisedly here, because to be unaffected by others and totally in control was thought to be fully masculine.)

In any case, this nonecological, nonrelational view of existence has had diverse negative consequences. One is the ecological crisis itself, especially the various forms of pollution. By assuming that things did not really enter into each other, and that "change" was simply the rearrangement of interchangeable parts (as in a machine), the modern world was not sensitive to the possibilities of irreversible change.

Another consequence has been that we have thought of ourselves as totally independent, autonomous individuals, who could realize our own good apart from the good of others and of the good of the whole. In fact, the conviction behind the competitiveness of modern life is that I can realize my good precisely by *defeating* yours! One task of the postmodern vision is to create a consciousness of our interdependence upon each other—of the profound degree to which it is true that the good of one individual is not separable from the good of the whole of which he or she is a part. (Some forms of thought called *postmodern* insist that we have to give up the notion of distinct individuals entirely. But this move would also falsify reality. Whitehead shows how radical relationality is compatible with radical individuality. It is only modern individual*ism* that must go.) Participants in this postmodern vision would immediately sense that working for the good of others, and for the whole (the whole community, the whole nation, the whole world), is working for their own good. This vision would not demand the unrealistic altruism thought by nonrelational moderns to be the ideal for human existence, that is, that we love and serve others *rather than* ourselves. By recognizing how we are all members of one another, the postmodern ethic would simply encourage us to follow the Biblical injunction to love others *as* ourselves.

Modernity has thought all this "love stuff" to be irrelevant to international politics. Realism, it has said, entails that politics be based solely upon power and self-interest. But what is *true* realism depends upon what reality is like, and in particular what the reality of human nature is. The modern assumption has been that people are what they are, regardless of the particular relations they are in. We characterize our "enemies" as *inherently* deceitful, bent on world domination, and so on. But on the basis of a relational view, we would expect that these others would feel, think, and behave differently, depending upon how we, *their* erstwhile enemies, are behaving. Just as we are literally different people, to some extent, depending upon with whom we are associating, the leaders of other nations will be literally different, depending upon the type of people they are dealing with. By stressing that we are not totally autonomous substances, unaffected internally by our relations with others, postmodern thought encourages a mentality that would be more flexible in its approach to international relations and more hopeful of the possibility that cooperation would replace conflict. It is precisely in our relations with other human beings, of course, that our prophecies are most self-fulfilling. If we expect the worst from others and act accordingly, that is precisely what we will get. Postmodern thought would not encourage naivete; it knows the widespread power of sin, especially as reinforced by the modern paradigm. But it would encourage us to look for good from our erstwhile "enemies," and to comport ourselves in ways most likely to allow that good to be manifested. By stressing a relational, ecological understanding of all existence, especially human existence, a postmodern view will help us realize that what other people are is partly a function of their environment, and that *we* are part of that environment.

There is yet another way in which the modern paradigm, with its non-ecological approach to reality, has contributed to world problems. By not focusing on the way each thing is affected by everything else, the modern paradigm has encouraged a piecemeal approach to solving problems. The "side-effects" of solutions have, therefore, often created more difficulty than the original problems. This feature of the postmodern consciousness is summarized in one of the slogans of the ecology movement: "You can't do just one thing." The rise of the ecological movement has made us more aware of the interconnectedness of all things, and also of our need to live in harmony with our *total* environment. We cannot project visions of social justice that depend upon having all the people on the planet come up to the material standard of living currently enjoyed by the average U. S. citizen: intolerable pollution, the depletion of all natural resources, global shortages of food and water, and surely nuclear catastrophe would result long before the goal could be reached, even if the energy problem could be solved.

Postmodern thought is ecological through and through, and provides the philosophical and theological grounding for the lasting insights popularized by the ecology movement. If it, in fact, becomes the basis for the new paradigm of our culture, future generations of citizens will *grow up* with an ecological consciousness in which the value of all things is respected and the interconnectedness of all things is recognized. The awareness that we must walk gently through the world, using only what we need, preserving the ecological balance for our neighbors and future generations, will be "common sense."

This ethic will be as basic to the religion of these postmodern humans as the drive to acquire possessions and dominate nature has been to the citizens of the modern world. World citizens with such an attitude will have a much better chance of living in peace with themselves and each other.

Those who are working for a transition to a postmodern paradigm are doing so because this transition (1) will serve to move us closer to the truth of things; (2) is necessary for our physical, moral, and spiritual health, as individuals and as communities; and (3) is probably necessary for our very survival. Some of them are persons who have focused their professional work primarily on the question of *truth*, for example, physicists, chemists, biologists, anthropologists, historians. Others have focused as well on the question of the way we *ought* to order our lives, for example, ethicists, political theorists, economists, psychotherapists, sociologists, theologians, philosophers. The task is to combine forces to develop a new *worldview* that their contemporaries and especially the rising generation will find convincing and also to begin spelling out the *new ethic*, the new way of ordering our individual, communal, national, and international relations, so as to provide realistic hope that it will lead to a better form of life. The Center for a Postmodern World came into being to promote this effort.

If this effort succeeds, so that postmodern thought of this sort becomes the foundation of the postmodern paradigm (just as the substance thought of Descartes, Newton, and others became the foundation of the modern paradigm), the human beings of future generations will not regard relations based upon coercive power as the "natural" and only "realistic" way to get things done; they will not regard nature as a "disenchanted" realm which is not akin to us and whose only value lies in its being a "natural resource" for us; their *real* religion will not consist in the drive to dominate nature and acquire material goods; they will not believe that human satisfaction comes primarily through money and the things it buys, and hence will not believe that economic considerations should be paramount in our public life; and they will not envisage the world as comprising autonomous atoms, and hence will not assume that problems can be solved in a piecemeal fashion, nor that the good of one individual or community can be attained in isolation from the good of all. They will have a sense of the Divine as permeating all things and as working persuasively in each part for the good of the whole. Their religious drive to imitate deity will lead them to make cooperative persuasion their chief *modus operandi* and habitually to look for ways to mesh their own good with the good of the whole.

NOTES

1. The idea of the "naturalistic fallacy," as formulated by G. E. Moore, was importantly motivated by the commendable desire to undermine Social Darwinism. Moore and others wanted to deny the ethical view that, because nonhuman nature operated in a wholly amoral way, and achieved progress by ruthlessly eliminating the weak, human beings ought to act in the same way. The widespread acceptance among ethicists that it is logically fallacious to derive human morality from the nature of things, however, has done nothing to change the fact that human beings do so. Rather than attacking the connection between is and ought, reality and morality, postmodern thought seeks to spread a new understanding of reality, from which will follow a better morality.

2. Carl Becker, *The Heavenly City of the Eighteenth-Century Philosophers* (New Haven, Conn.: Yale University Press, 1932), 63. In a similar vein, Whitehead has said: "Whatever suggests a cosmology, suggests a religion" (*Religion in the Making* [Cleveland: World Publishing Company, 1960], 141).

3. This type of postmodernism is diametrically opposed to eliminative postmodernism on this point. For example, Richard Rorty rejects the existence of any ahistorical principles, such as divine character or will or intrinsic human dignity and rights, which make certain types of behavior inherently immoral. But he wants us to treat each other kindly, saying that as a "free-loading atheist" he gratefully invokes Judeo-Christian principles. Like Hume before him, who wanted to leave "practice" unaffected by "theory," Rorty wants the denial of any foundations for the moral life to remain "merely philosophical," having no effect upon how we act. See "Postmodernist Bourgeois Liberalism," *Journal of Philosophy* 80 (1983), 583-89, esp. 588–89.

4. See John C. Greene, *Science, Ideology, and World View* (Berkeley: University of California Press, 1981); Richard Hofstadter, *Social Darwinism in American Thought* (Philadelphia: University of Pennsylvania Press, 1944).

5. See Paul K. Feyerabend, *Against Method* (London: NLB Verso, 1978), 218; *Science in a Free Society* (London: NLB, 1978), 73.

6. See Carolyn Merchant, *The Death of Nature: Women, Ecology, and the Scientific Revolution* (San Francisco: Harper & Row, 1980).

7. *Ibid.*, chaps. 7–10.

8. See Carl Becker, *The Heavenly City of the Eighteenth-Century Philosophers*; John B. Bury, *The Idea of Progress: An Inquiry into its Origin and Growth* (New York: Macmillan, 1920).

9. See Morris Berman, *The Reenchantment of the World* (Ithaca, N. Y.: Cornell University Press, 1981).

NOTES ON CONTRIBUTORS
AND CENTERS

JOHN B. COBB, JR., is author of *Process Theology as Political Theology*, coauthor of *The Liberation of Life: From the Cell to the Community*, and coeditor of *Process Philosophy and Social Thought*. He is the Ingraham professor of theology at the School of Theology at Claremont, Avery professor of religion at Claremont Graduate school, and director of the Center for Process Studies, 1325 North College, Claremont, Calif. 91711.

HERMAN E. DALY is author of *Toward a Steady-State Economy* and *Steady-State Economics* and editor of *Economics, Ecology, Ethics: Essays Toward a Steady-State Economy*. He is professor of economics at Louisiana State University, Baton Rouge, La. 70803.

RICHARD A. FALK is author of *The End of World Order, A Study of Future Worlds*, and *Revolutionaries and Functionaries: The Dual Face of Terrorism*. He is the Albert G. Milbank professor of international law and practice at Princeton University, Princeton, N. J. 08544.

FREDERICK FERRÉ is author of *Logic, Language, and God, Basic Modern Philosophy of Religion, Shaping the Future: Resources for the Post-modern World,* and *Philosophy of Technology*. He is chairman of the Department of Philosophy, University of Georgia, Athens, Ga. 30602.

C. DEAN FREUDENBERGER is author of *Christian Responsibility in a Hungry World* and *Food for Tomorrow?* He teaches international development studies and missions at the School of Theology at Claremont, Claremont, Calif. 91711.

DAVID RAY GRIFFIN is author of *God, Power, and Evil* and *Process Theology* (with John Cobb) and editor of *Physics and the Ultimate Significance of Time* and *The Reenchantment of Science*. He is professor of philosophy of religion at the School of Theology at Claremont and Claremont Graduate School, founding president of the Center for a Postmodern World in Santa Barbara, and executive director of the Center for Process Studies, 1325 North College, Claremont, Calif. 91711.

JOE HOLLAND is author of *Social Analysis: Linking Faith and Justice* (with Peter Henriot) and many occasional papers available through the Center of Concern, 3700 13th Street, N.E., Washington, D. C. 20017. He is director of the American Catholic Lay Network in Washington, D. C., and executive director of PILLAR (Pallottine Institute for Lay Leadership and Apostolate Research), Presidents Hall, Seton Hall University, South Orange, N. J. 07079.

CATHERINE KELLER is author of *From a Broken Web: Separation, Sexism, and Self.* She teaches theology at The Theological School, Drew University, Madison, N. J. 07940.

CHARLENE SPRETNAK is author of *The Lost Goddesses of Early Greece, The Spiritual Dimension of Green Politics,* and *Green Politics: The Global Promise* (with Fritjof Capra) and editor of *The Politics of Women's Spirituality.* She receives mail at P.O. Box 9997, Berkeley, Calif. 94709.

This series is published under the auspices of the Center for a Postmodern World and the Center for Process Studies.

The Center for a Postmodern World is an independent nonprofit organization in Santa Barbara, California, founded by David Ray Griffin. It promotes the awareness and exploration of the postmodern worldview and encourages reflection about a postmodern world, from postmodern art, spirituality, and education to a postmodern world order, with all this implies for economics, ecology, and security. One of its major projects is to produce a collaborative study that marshals the numerous facts supportive of a postmodern worldview and provides a portrayal of a postmodern world order toward which we can realistically move. It is located at 2060 Alameda Padre Serra, Suite 101, Santa Barbara, California 93103.

The Center for Process Studies is a research organization affiliated with the School of Theology at Claremont and Claremont University Center and Graduate School. It was founded by John B. Cobb, Jr., Director, and David Ray Griffin, Executive Director. It encourages research and reflection upon the process philosophy of Alfred North Whitehead, Charles Hartshorne, and related thinkers, and upon the application and testing of this viewpoint in all areas of thought and practice. This center sponsors conferences, welcomes visiting scholars to use its library, and publishes a scholarly journal, *Process Studies,* and a quarterly *Newsletter.* It is located at 1325 North College, Claremont, California 91711.

Both centers gratefully accept (tax-deductible) contributions to support their work.

INDEX

157